To Plan

or

Not to Plan

?

A Comprehensive-Master Business Plan
With an elaborate Mergers & Acquisitions segment

Dr. John N. Kalaras, Ph.D.

This Master Plan
is the property of

First name: _____ MI _____

Last: _____

Date acquired: _____

Personal Info: _____

All people are gifted

Some open their packages earlier than others

I have just opened mine

A note to the reader

In this book you will find

Five major segments with a total of 90 specific issues covering every possible concern of a well-designed Business Plan.

In addition you will discover an elaborate and very unique coverage of Mergers and Acquisitions.

A sixteen-page rubric that addresses:

- Basic concerns of M & A's
- Financial Issues
- Legal Issues
- Marketing Issues
- Quality Issues
- Information Technology and Security
- Policies and Procedures
- Organizational Issues
- Miscellaneous concerns

To Plan or Not to Plan

The Plan never failed us, we failed to plan

Therefore we planned to fail by default!

Every authentic manuscript bears the hand-written signature of the author.

Dedicated

To all my students

Who should always remember

The Plan never failed us

We failed to plan

Therefore we planned to fail by default

About the Author

Dr. John N. Kalaras is a Global Speaker on Quality and Leadership.
He studied Quality all his life, but made the study of Quality his life!

Senior Professor-Senior Global Consultant and founder of

QUALITY TRAINING INSTITUTE

Honored by THE COUNCIL OF EUROPE-UNESCO as

THE HONORARY PROFESSOR OF THE YEAR 1999

He also has a

White House Recognition on Academic Excellence, while he served on the
President's Business Advisory Council responsible for academic issues in USA 2005-2009

Additional works of the Author

Career Success (College textbook) ISBN: 147 8280 697 at Amazon.com

Your Passport to Quality (College textbook)
Continuous Improvement through Leadership (adopted and used by DePaul University)
Leadership and Service Excellence (adopted and used by Hoopis University of Northwest Mutual)
The Scandalous Professor (Novel, based on a true story)

BUSINESS PROGRAMS-WORKSHOPS

Business Basics	*Executive Level Leadership-Coaching*
Project Management	*Excellence in Client Service*
Fundamentals of Quality	*Hospitality Excellence*
Lean-Six Sigma / Yellow Belt	*Effective Change in the Work Place*
Green Belt / Black Belt	*MRP/CRP and Facility Planning*
Introduction to Leadership (Academic version)	*Career Planning I & II*
Leadership Fundamentals (Business version)	*Transition your Career Successfully*

All rights reserved ©2012

MY PLEDGE

I am a wise professional,

Therefore:

Before I speak, I shall listen

Before I write or sign, I shall think

Before I spend, I shall earn

Before I invest, I shall investigate

Before I criticize I shall critique

Before I pray, I shall forgive

Before I act, I shall study

Before I quit, I shall try

Before I retire, I shall save

And

Before I depart, I shall give!

FOOD FOR THOUGHT

All people are gifted;

Some open their packages earlier than others.

You have just opened yours!

♦

It is individuals who receive trophies

But it takes a team to bring home the Championship

We build championship teams!

♦

If you think you can or you cannot, you are right!

♦

If you do what you have always done,

You will get what you have always gotten.

Try change, creativity and innovation," They do a mind good"!

♦

Experience is a hard teacher;
She gives the test first and the lesson afterwards!

♦

Success comes before work only in a dictionary!

Table of Contents

Item #	Description	Page #
	Introduction	16
	INTRODUCTORY-BASIC TOPICS	17
1	Executive Summary	17
2	Vision Statement	18
3	Mission Statement	19
4	Quality Statement	19
5	Code of Ethics	19
6	The Type of Business we are in	20
7	Our Products	20
8	Our competition and competitive edge	20
9	Strategic partners	21
10	Management team and professional advisors	21
	Check point	22
	MARKETING	25
11	What is your Marketing philosophy	27
12	Market Strategy, Market share, Growth strategies, PR, Advertising	28
13	Market analysis: Segmentation, Targeting, Positioning, Pricing, Demographics	29
14	Describe your target market and market niche	30
15	Overview of your products/services	30
16	What's coming next	30
17	Customer demographics	32
18	Where are our growth opportunities	32
19	Stages of market development	32
20	New Challenges	33
21	Industry trends: Can you perform a competitive-trend analysis on the following?	33
22	Product/service	34
23	Price	34
24	Image/style/design	34
25	Quality	35
26	Perceived value	35
27	Brand recognition	35
28	Customer relationships	36
29	Delivery time of product/service	36
30	Convenience of use	37
31	Credit policies	37
32	Customer/client service	38
33	Social consciousness	38
34	Product mix/line	39
35	Projected Market Share and Market Growth	39
36	Operational Efficiency, Effectiveness and Productivity	39
37	Operational Costs (high-medium-low)	40
38	Technological Competence-IT/Web	40
39	Patents/Trademarks/Copyrights	40

Item #	Description	Page #
40	Creative ability	40
41	Innovative ability	41
42	SWOT or SCOT analysis	41
	SWOT Chart	42
	Competitive Analysis Chart	43
	OPERATIONAL CONSIDERATIONS	45
43	Introduction/People	47
44	Capital Equipment (also called Fixed Assets)	49
45	Procedures /Operations	49
46	Engineers and R&D	50
47	Benchmarking, ISO series	50
48	Learning curve	51
49	People, training / development	51
50	Risks	51
51	QC tools and Fish-Bone Diagram	52
	Useful graphs and charts	53
52	Top-down/Bottom-up approach and Tall /Flat hierarchy	54
53	Layout considerations	54
54	Location concerns	54
55	Team building and self-directed teams	55
56	Core competencies	55
57	Outsourcing	55
58	Groupthink vs Brainstorming	57
59	Conflict resolution	57
60	Capacity concerns	57
61	Machinery and Equipment	58
62	Logistics, Supply-Chain Management	58
63	Policies, Procedures and Manuals	59
64	Forecasting	60
65	MRP / CRP	60
66	Scheduling: Forward-Backward	61
	FINNCIAL CONSIDERATIONS	63
67	Overview of Financial statements and projections	65
	67.a-67.q	65-69
68	Budgeting and funds needed	70
69	Types of costs	70
70	Start-up Costs and Investments	70
71	BEP, Payback Period & NPV	71
72	Make-or-Buy decisions	71
73	ND-NC-NC Agreement	72
	PROJECT MANAGEMENT	73
74	The Business Plan is a Project	75
75	Project Portfolio	75
76	The role of the Project Manager and Scope of project	76
77	Develop the Project Plan	76

Item #	Description	Page #
78	Project stakeholders	76
79	ID activities and their duration, WBS and deliverables	77
80	Develop the HR Requirements and the Project Schedule	77
81	Project Management and Communication	78
82	Estimate Resource Requirements, Project Budget and Cost Estimates.	79
83	Plan Inputs, Tools & Techniques, Outputs	79
84	Project Network	80
85	Develop the project team and assign responsibilities	81
86	Risk Management, Quantitative & Qualitative Analysis	83
87	Risk and Uncertainty	83
88	Risk Register, Management and Response	83
89	Procurements, Acquisitions and Outsourcing	84
90	Mergers and Acquisitions	86
	MERGERS & ACQUISITIONS	87
	Basic Issues	88
	Finance	89
	Organizational Issues	95
	Policies and Procedures	96
	Information Technology/Security	96
	Miscellaneous concerns	97
	Quality Issues	98
	Marketing Issues	101
	Legal Issues	102
	APPENDICES	105
	Useful Graphs and Charts	106
	A. GANTT Chart, B. Interrelationships Chart C. Process Diagram	106
	D. Matrix Diagram, E. Decision Tree	107
	F. PERT or Network Diagram G. Bottleneck Diagram H. Process Diagram	108
	I. Affinity Diagram, J. Decision Tree with Expected Values	109
	K. WBS L. Computerized Flowchart	110
	L. Team Member Relationship and Evaluation Form	111
	M. Multiple Trend Analysis Graphs	112
	Notes	113
	N. Organizational Chart	114
	Notes	115
	O. SPC Chart P. Capabilities Improvement Chart	116
	Balance Sheet	117
	Income Statement	118
	Cash-Flow Statement	119
	Market Segmentation Worksheets	121
	Practice your Financial Statements here	122
	A checklist of basic issues	123
	Worksheet	124
	Business Plan Outline	125-127
	A note from the author	128

A COMPREHENSIVE-MASTER BUSINESS PLAN

Introduction

A Business Plan (BP) is a formal, written document that provides a stethoscopic analysis and presentation of an organization's past, current and future activities.

A good Business Plan should be comprehensive enough to address all possible future issues and of course it should provide a crystal clear picture of the current status of the business, along with what has happened in the past. For "start-ups" where you don't have a "past" for the business, we will suggest a slightly different version. However, keep in mind that you definitely have a "past" of the person(s) behind the proposed business.

In writing this book we were enormously attentive to any and hopefully all possible issues or concerns that a comprehensive and all inclusive Business Plan should incorporate. We are fully aware of the fact that not everyone will have a need for all elements incorporated in this Master Business Plan. However, we have provided more than enough subjects-areas so that every probable need has been addressed. We expect that you go through the entire content and then identify the topics you are interested in incorporating into your Business Plan. This manual serves as a template or a guide. Customize it to fit your specific objective and individual needs.

Before we proceed with the design of our Business Plan we should first define its purpose. What do we want to accomplish with it? Next, it's critically important that we are aware of who will be the recipient or user of such plan. From this perspective, Business Plans are classified into:

-External users (Financial institutions, investors, donors and other entities)

-Internal users (Strategic, Operational, Expansion, Marketability)

If we are preparing it for **Bankers**, we should pay special attention to the following:

- Financial Statements and requested amount
- Where, when and how will the funds be used
- Repayment plan and time table (you may need a two year grace period)
- Collateral assets
- Co-signer(s)

If our intent to present it to potential **Investors**, the following are crucial topics:

- Amount of funds to be raised
- Vehicle for raising such funds, i.e. bonds, stocks, loans, type of stocks etc
- If stocks are used, will dividends be paid, when, how
- If bonds are used, what interest will be paid, maturity date etc
- When the funds will be needed and in what amounts
- How the funds will be used (operational-infrastructure-expansion or other)

- Potentiality of success, how and why
- Overall estimated ROI
- Estimated Payback period and Break-Even Point
- Partial repayment via IPO
- Financial reporting methods along with who will be doing such reporting
- Possible involvement of investors in the decision making such as Board of Directors

Finally, you may want a Business Plan to serve as a "blueprint" for your own internal planning and operational needs. Regardless of the purpose, we have prepared an all-inclusive blueprint.

Of course, another important factor is the type of business we are dealing with. It makes a difference if our business is a **manufacturing**, a **merchandizing** or a **service** entity. In manufacturing, most of the capital should go to machinery and equipment. In merchandizing, attention should be given to the merchandise purchased and sold (inventory turnover ratio). Finally, in service, we don't need much capital for infrastructure, but our payroll will be considerably high. It's obvious that defining the audience is critically important. Regardless of the type of Business Plan it's significant that the following are clearly addressed:

1. **Benefit to the community**: How will our product/service better serve it?

2. **Economic benefit**: Here we should stress the career opportunities (jobs) that will be created along with the support to surrounding business. For instance, if we are building a university, other businesses in the area such as restaurants will be positively affected.

3. **Human Intelligence Development**: Here we should demonstrate that we won't only use our people's knowledge, but we will help them grow and develop through training and education.

Structurally and organizationally we have identified the following major sections.

- a) Introductory-basic topics
- b) Marketing Considerations
- c) Operational Requirements
- d) Financial-Capital Requirements
- e) Project Management
- f) Mergers and Acquisitions
- g) Appendices, Graphs & Charts

INTRODUCTORY-BASIC TOPICS

1. Executive summary

Here we should develop a three to four paragraph statement that clearly describes who we are, what we do, where we want or should be in the future and how it should be accomplished. The executive summary should not exceed the two pages. Exceptions may be made if the project is really large and complex. Regardless of its length, the Executive Summary should provide a

compelling story about the concept. If we are presenting to a group of potential investors, the Plan should "grab" their attention and create immediate interest. That's why we should address only the most important points of our proposed concept. Things like the uniqueness of our products or service, the type of clientele we are after and of course why and how the project will succeed.

In addition we should justify all the "how to and why." Issues like the composition and capabilities of our executive team and organizational approach, our management team and its style, capital requirements and payback period or ROI future projections and potential success. We should also address the industry we want to be in; is it a growing one, what direction do we think it is headed, in both, the short and long term? How are we prepared for this and how well our organization is positioned to play a leading role? Finally we should address the legal form of our business, along with why we selected such form i.e. Sole Proprietorship, Partnership, Corporation, LLC, and the benefit to the investor(s). In demonstrating this, make sure that enthusiasm and professionalism is embedded throughout our presentation.

Checkpoint.
 A successful Executive Summary should address the following questions.
Do we:
- ➤ Have a compelling story?
- ➤ Create an immediate and strong interest?
- ➤ Have a crystal clear description of our products/services?
- ➤ Define the Location, the Market and the Competition adequately?
- ➤ Demonstrate and justify the benefits clearly?
- ➤ Ask for a reasonable and justifiable amount of funds?
- ➤ Describe the industry and its direction/trend?
- ➤ Demonstrate a Leadership role?
- ➤ Present a qualified executive team and other personnel?
- ➤ Describe and justify the form of business?

2. Vision statement

The Vision Statement is one that states where our organization should be in 10 to 20 years and beyond. It reflects the long-term outlook of our business. The question that is usually asked and should be answered is: *Where do we want to be in 20 years from now?* The Vision Statement embodies our

philosophy and the overall purpose of going into business. Indirectly here is where we show our values, our guiding principles and the ultimate destination.

3. Mission statement

In the Mission Statement we should show **how** we are going to materialize the Vision shown above. Here we will outline the major steps that should be followed. If the Vision Statement addresses the "WHAT" the Mission Statement should address the "HOW and WHY." A Mission Statement may include Goals, Objectives, Projects and Tasks we intend to perform in order to achieve the Vision.

4. Quality statement

In this statement we should state the level of Quality we want to achieve and maintain in our organization, along with how and why we will continue improving it. Things like achieving and maintaining operational excellence may be part of the statement. Important issue to remember is that "Quality" is defined by our customers and is implemented and improved by our associates. Each employee "owns" her/his portion of Quality that goes into our product or service. And that should be clearly shown in this statement.

5. Code of Conduct-Ethics

We all know what is right or wrong. Regardless of culture, economic condition, geographic location, gender and any other possible determinant characteristic, Ethics and Ethical behavior are imperative to the health, success and continued growth of any organization. Code of Ethics should NOT consist of lists of what people should or should not do. From the moment we compile a list, you are running the risk to not include everything, therefore we open a window to "opportunists" and the "unethical" to violate the code of Ethics and get away with it. We suggest that a Code of Conduct-Ethics should read something like: *We have trained and educated our associates on Ethics and Ethical behavior and we expect them to exercise their judgment in doing what is morally right at all times.*

A Code of Ethics could and should be very straight forward and simple. Writing something like: *We expect all of our associates to do what is legally, morally and ethically right at all times.*

We suggest that you ask your associates to compose their own version of a Code of Ethics.

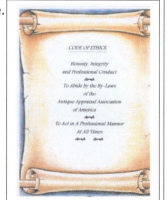

6. The type of business we are in

When people start a business or buy an existing one, i.e. a furniture store, they think that they are in the furniture business. When they open a travel agency, they believe that they are in the traveling business. We have a different and unique approach to defining the business we are in. And that could make our Business Plan a unique one, definitely different from the rest. All of us should understand that the business we are in is:

To serve our clients in the best way possible, hopefully better that our competition, with the goal to elevate them to the point of Loyal Client, via the products or services we offer.

Once we internalize this mentality and act on it accordingly, we should surpass the level of mere satisfaction and elevate the relationship with our clients to that of a Loyal Client. This is easier said than done. It takes forever to build this kind of relationship, but it's definitely achievable.

7. Our products

Do we know what products and/or services we offer? Do we know what products and services we "sell" to what markets or customers? Do we have main categories of products? Do we have by-products, that are the result of a process, but we overlook to mention them?
According to the Boston Consulting Group we should mention which products are the "cash cows-stars-question marks-dogs." We need to describe in detail at least the major products we offer, their technical specifications, their distribution or delivery requirements, drawings of products and processes, how competitive our products are, and their overall potentiality of success. Technical specifications, drawings and photos may be shown in the Appendices. Finally, product lines and product mix should also be mentioned. The most crucial mistake businesses make about their products/services is that they stress the attributes of the produce/service, not realizing that the customer is primarily interested in the product's benefits and secondly in its attributes. Our Business Plan should make that distinction and it should emphasize how the customer will benefit from it, rather than what the product offers or can do.

8. Our competition and competitive edge

Do we know our competition? Do we know our top 2-3 competitors? What percent of the market do we possess? What is their market share? Where is our competitive advantage? How long will it stay as an advantage? Do we know what are our most important company strengths and core competencies? What factors will make the company succeed? What do we think our major competitive strengths are? What background experience, skills and strengths do we and our management team bring to this new venture? These are critical questions that should be addressed by the Business Plan.

9. Strategic partners

Every business should have at least 3-5 strategic partners. A strategic partner is another separate and different entity that shares the same philosophy, interests, and ambitions, and wants to grow and succeed along with us. A strategic partner is NOT a competitor or necessarily a customer. It's another business that could be complementing ours or result to a mutual benefit from each other's co-existence. An example may be a grocery store chain "partners" with a bank. There is a mutual benefit for both, the bank and the grocery store. Strategic partners don't look for immediate profit, rather they try to build long-term mutually beneficial relationships. In our Business Plan we will show the type of Strategic Partners we are engaged with.

10. Management team and professional advisors

Every organization has its own management team members who are responsible for the effective execution of the organization's vision, mission and objectives. What happens frequently is that the management team members become so deeply overwhelmed and involved with the daily, many times difficult decisions, they lose sight of the "big picture". *They see the trees but they can't see the forest.* Sometimes they even lose their objectivity; and this is natural. It happens because they are emotionally attached to the issues. They know their people and the struggles they are facing. So when a manager has to let an employee go, many times, this presents a difficult and sometimes an emotional dilemma. It's obvious that impartiality, objectivity and detachment need to be in place. In addition to this, the management team might lose or bypass an opportunity, simply because they didn't have the chance to come across it.

In order for such syndromes to be alleviated we use Professional Advisors. Such people, just like the management team, are experts in their field, with one "*minor*" difference": They are unbiased and most importantly they are dealing with similar situations like ours in other organizations almost every day.

Having seen how other organizations have addressed the issues we are dealing with now, they are usually able to provide solid and useful advice.

Every organization should have a team of professional advisors. Such teams usually consist of people who have expertise in: Finance, Marketing, Law, Operations, HR, Foreign Markets-Investments, Mergers/Acquisitions and R&D, to mention a few. We feel that this is an important concern, that's why we have devoted a segment to it.

Checkpoint

We would close this introductory part by asking the questions/issues that follow:

- **General concerns**
- What's the purpose of this plan? (Operating guide or Financial proposal)
- What's the business organizational structure (provide organizational chart)
- What's the business legal structure (is it a corporation, or a partnership)
- Who is (are) the principle(s)
- Why will we be successful
- Primarily what business are we in; service, merchandise, manufacture etc.
- What is our "niche" or competitive advantage
- Status of the business; is it a start-up or existing.
- If it's an existing business, how long has it been in operation

- **Is this A NEW BUSINESS; if so**
- What is our experience in this field
- Do we have any affidavits of support from potential vendors
- Why will we be successful
- Have we investigated possible major obstacles and business risks
- Could we show credit worthiness in the form of "line of credit" or other financial vehicles
- When will the business be ready to operate
- How long will we need until we are ready for operation i.e. will it take six months to build it

- **If this is A TAKE-OVER of an existing business**
- What stage of the business-life-cycle is the business at
- Is this a hostile take-over, a merger, an acquisition
- What's the purpose of the take-over (expansion, profitability, market dominance)
- If it's not a hostile take-over, why is the Seller selling
- What is the right acquisition price
- Who and how will appraise the business; what's a fair market value
- How will we pay for the business; cash-out-right, partial payment/partial ownership
- How will we make the business more efficient, productive and profitable

NOTES

Marketing Considerations

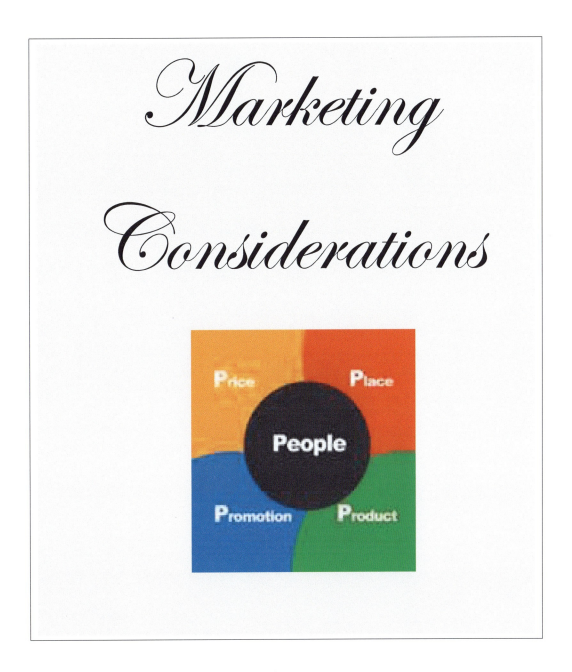

MARKETING

Effective Marketing is the key to success of any business. Regardless of the type of product or service we offer, without a successful Marketing approach chances are that we may fail. Successful Marketing begins with defining and understanding the organization's philosophy and next by performing a scientifically proper research. Both of these major topics are explained below.

11. What is our Marketing philosophy

There are several acceptable-known Marketing philosophies; which one is ours? Marketing, the way we know it today, has gone through several stages or eras. During the "Production Era" products were scarce and the notion was that the products will sell by themselves. There was no need for advertising or promotional efforts the way we know them today.

Then came the "Sales Era" where companies would hire more salespeople to promote, distribute and sell their products; competition started to appear on the horizon.

Next evolved the "Marketing Concept Era" during which the slogan: *we are in business to satisfy our customer's needs and wants*, became the driving force of most marketing activities.

Presently we are in what most experts call the "**Customer Era**" with an important outgrowth of this focus resulted to what we call: **Customer Relationship Marketing-CRM**.

Please realize that not all companies are at this level yet. However, if we want to be competitive and under the assumption that many of our competitors perform CRM, we should at least be doing the same.

Actually what we suggest is a level of Marketing that goes beyond all of these.
We call it   **VALUE-LOYALTY MARKETING**.

This type of Marketing realizes that creating "satisfied" customers isn't enough. A satisfied customer is exactly that: Satisfied for the moment. Nothing prevents a satisfied customer from looking elsewhere for better service, price, reliability and consistency. Therefore our customer may be satisfied today, but we have no guarantee if that customer would still be there tomorrow. Our **Value-Loyalty Marketing** concept creates loyal clients, fully realizing that a loyal client will be with you "forever." A loyal client has developed trust and confidence in our product/service and of course such trust expands to our business as a whole. It's vitally important that we do everything within our ability to create such an environment. It takes willingness to go the extra mile, it requires that we constantly innovate, create and enhance what we are already doing well. We call that "Delighting the customer with the unexpected." However, we need to remember that today's delighters become tomorrow's expectation. Therefore innovation becomes a journey not a destination. More on this follows later. The next issue we will address here is **VALUE**. What's the value to the customer? Does s/he find **VALUE** in what we offer? That's why we pay attention not only to the attributes but mainly to the **BENEFITS** of our product/service. Customers may care less for the attributes of a product or service. What they are interested in is the **BENEFITS** of it.

12. Market Strategy

Once the Marketing Philosophy is determined, we should then establish our strategy that will help us conquer the market. Such Strategy serves a fundamental purpose that allows organizations to develop opportunities that will increase sales and achieve a sustainable competitive advantage. Basic elements included in the Marketing Strategy could be:

12-1 Market Research: Regardless of how well you know an area it is dangerous to assume that you know the potential market and the way it behaves or will behave. That's why we strongly suggest that we perform a Market Research. Such research will give us an insight from the customer's point of view that will be current, pertinent and accurate. More on how a Market Research should be conducted will be presented more analytically in the appropriate segment.

12-2 Market Share: We should know what market share we currently possess and where we want to be by the end of the year or by the end of my 5-10 year plan. For a start-up we should have in mind a "desired" percent that we should aim for.

12-3 Branding: Remember the following profound statement. *If you don't Brand your company or products others will Brand them for you.* A very risky thought. Therefore Branding becomes imperative. Branding may be expressed in the form of Brand Equity, Brand Loyalty and Brand Awareness.

12-4 Growth Strategies: There are several different Growth Strategies; for instance we may attempt to grow our business with the same products/services by entering new markets. On the other hand we could stay within the same markets but introduce new products. And of course we could do both, new products and new markets.

12-5 Promotion: In general, Promotion encompasses all the methods an organization will use to motivate people to purchase their product or service. Such methods may include Advertising, Personal Selling, Public Relations, Publicity and other promotional efforts. Our promotion should have a budget for start-up promotional activities and later for on-going promotion. Such budget is usually expressed as a percent of revenue or sales.

12-6 Advertising: This is an important function of our business. As in most cases, we should pay attention to what, why, how, when we advertise. We should also come to the realization that advertising is a science and a specialty. Especially in today's media bombardment we should attempt to be as effective as we possibly can. Many believe that any kind of advertising will be beneficial to the business, not realizing that the wrong way of advertising could be counterproductive. The message we would send through our advertising strategy should be effective and produce measurable results. In addition, attention should be paid to what we want to advertise, the company or the product(s). Each has its own idiosyncrasies.

12-7 Public Relations (PR): This is a crucial element in our business. PR is intended to create a positive image and a favorite climate about our organization. We should pay attention not only to what we do or say but mainly to how we say it, who is saying it, when it is said and why. If we can effectively answer these "questions" we should be able to develop an excellent PR strategy. Keep in mind that what the message conveys and what the prospect perceives may be two different things.

We should also understand that many times people don't act according to reality but according to their perception of reality.

12-8 Sales Promotion: Given that a Sales Promotion is a short term attempt to increase sales, we should definitely incorporate into our Business Plan the specific Sales Promotions we will be proposing. It's a stimulus that triggers customer interest-purchase by means of short-term incentives. Therefore we should state how frequently, for how long and for what specific products/services are we going to apply it.

12-9 Publicity: By definition, Publicity is any company-product information distributed to the public through media that is NOT paid for or controlled by the company. In other words, we deliberately attempt to influence the public's perception about our company, product or service.

The two main advantages of Publicity are the low cost, if any, and the credibility or impact it has, because it is communicated by a third party. The disadvantage is luck of control. Again, as with all attributes stated above, we should make it clear that in our Business Plan we should make provisions for Publicity.

13. *Market Analysis, including: Segmentation, Targeting, Positioning, Pricing, Demographics, Attributes and Benefits*

Studying and analyzing the market should be a continuous endeavor. By studying we will learn past market behaviors, which may assist on taking the proper actions now and in the future. By analyzing we will obtain a better understanding of why such behaviors occurred. In general, when we know the "who" the "what" and the "why" we should be able to take actions that will bring the desired results. The specifics that we should look into are:

Market Segmentation, just like the term indicates, during Market Segmentation we identify smaller-manageable sections of the market, in order to study people's behavior in each section-segment. People say "divide and concur." Segmentation may take different forms. We could segment a market based on geographic criteria, or economic, or age, or gender, or level of education. A geographic segmentation may mean that we "segment" the market in North-South-East-West market segments. After the completion of the Market Segmentation we should proceed with the function of Targeting.

Targeting, is equivalent to using a microscope to carefully look into the elements of our population sample. Remember, we have already identified a segment, during the previous stage. Here we look into the specific composition of the segment and then we identify the people with the highest potentiality to purchase our product or service. This activity is directly related to ROI. The more accurate we are with the identification of the proper potential buyers, the higher the return on our investment in this function. To better comprehend this let's presume that during the segmentation we decided to work with the East geographic segment. Now that we have the "boundaries" we could look for the specific potential clientele, such as people with income higher than $80,000. per year.

14. Describe our target market and market niche

In the previous section we addressed some significant Marketing issues. Along with them goes the importance of Market Niche. Identifying what makes us unique, where our strengths are and capitalizing on them is an important role that we should play. Having the right pricing policy or promotion or advertising is important; identifying a "niche" is crucial.

Here we should state not only our competitiveness but also our unique advantage in relation to our competitors. We call that the **"Market Nice."** Investors want to see if there is one because it increases the potentiality for success. In other words, what is the single attribute we have that others don't?

15. Overview of our products/services

Here we should enlist all of our products/services by category and individually. In addition to "listing" we should also continuously examine how our products/services behave. A trend analysis of product behavior over time is a good approach. This way we will know which products are "cash-cows" or "stars" or "question marks" or even "dogs" according to the Boston Group Analysis. Observing the behavior of the market, identifying new trends or products and adjusting our production accordingly should be an on-going endeavor. This is best executed by adopting continuous product/service addition or deletion. And that should be clearly shown in the Plan.

16. What's coming next?

With one eye on our internal processes and the other on the future, we should constantly look into the:
- Market and its trends
- Competition
- Economy and Technology
- Interest rate behavior
- Inflation
- Currency exchange rate
- Unemployment rate and several other factors, both internal and external, that have a direct or indirect impact on to our business.

Basically, we should behave like the Roman God Janus, with the two faces; one looking at past experiences and the other envisioning the future. If we want to have an impressive Business Plan we should do the same. Learn from the past and plan the future.

Distribution Channels is another essential element to be addressed by the Business Plan. Here we should answer questions regarding Wholesale or Retail, Vertical or Horizontal distribution, Centralized or Decentralized distribution, Wholesale Intermediaries or Retail Intermediaries, Web utilization, Agents or Brokers, Electronic Retailing, Telemarketing, Multilevel or Direct Selling. Of course this topic falls under the main category of Supply-Chain Management addressed further in this manual.

Positioning, deals with the way you launch your product or service. It's known that placing a product in the market at the right time is important. The way you present the product is even more critical. Most people are only concerned with the way they launch their product in relation to the competition. Well, that's half the battle. The most critical element about Positioning is the way we present your product or service in relation to the rest of your products or services. We don't want to have success with the new product and "kill" the existing products. In closing, Positioning is defined as the proper launching of a product or service in relation to the competition and to the other products/services of an organization. If we don't pay attention to the impact on the rest of our products, we may be cannibalizing the existing products for the benefit of the new.

Pricing, should be the next major function. We have at least 15-18 pricing techniques. Some of them may be:
Competitive Pricing, where we price our products according to the competition
Cost-Plus, refers to a technique where we add a desired profit on top of the cost
Leader Pricing, refers to setting a price with the objective being to become the leading force in the market. Leading pricing results to high pricing
Low-End Pricing, applies the lowest possible price, which allows a new entrant to survive in the market, until the product or service becomes known. Later the price may increase
Skimming, is another technique which allows companies to take advantage of all possible buyers. It works as follows: A company will price a product at the highest possible price and once all potential buyers are exhausted the price will drop to the next level; once these potential buyers are exhausted then the company will do the same, until it reaches the lowest possible level of sale. This way the company explores and takes advantage of all potential buyers. It's a time consuming technique and it can't be applied to all organizations, however retail business like a clothier store could easily adopt this method.

Demographics

Once we identify our clientele base, we should then look into the clients' characteristics. Attributes like their specific location-geographic dispersion, income level, age, gender, education, social class, geographic density, occupation, ethnicity and religion, to mention a few. Depending upon the industry we are in, we should look for attributes specific to our industry. Obviously such demographic analysis will be influenced by our decision to sell B2B or B2C and the number on intermediaries that exist between us and the final client/user of our product or service.

Attributes and Benefits

When we present our Business Plan we should definitely differentiate between the product's "Attributes" and "Benefits."
As Attributes we understand any and all features incorporated in the product or service.
As Benefits we understand the features and characteristics of a product that the client is willing to pay for; in other words what's important and useful to the client. If our product or service consists of features that aren't needed by the client, don't even emphasize them. You may offer them as extras at no cost to the client. Keep in mind that both, clients and investors are more interested in the Benefits and less in the Attributes. It's critical that we build features-attributes into our product so that we can sell the benefits.

17. Customer demographics

It was stated previously that knowing our customer base is significant. In here we attempt to obtain a better understanding of the customer base composition and its behavior. More specifically, in performing Market Segmentation and Targeting we should analyze and examine specific factors of our customer base; factors like age, occupation, gender, income level, race, ethnicity etc. This will allow us to identify who buys what, when, why and in what frequency or quantity. Knowing this, we can make better plans and predictions, which will allow us to function more effectively. Having the ability to plan and act accordingly, definitely makes us more productive and efficient in what we do.

18. Where are our growth opportunities

We have the responsibility to identify any and all possible areas of growth. Once we identify them, then we should prioritize them according to their significance and size. Let's explain what such areas of growth involve. A new geographic area could be more appealing in relation to a new product. In addition, the magnitude of the potential growth and its impact on to the bottom line or ROI should also be examined. Effect on bottom line and ROI could be two different issues; they will be explored in the appropriate segment under Financial Statements.

19. Stages of market development

Speaking of market growth and development, we should first explore and understand some fundamental issues. Market growth relates to market development, but they aren't the same. Market growth means we are enlarging our market. For instance, if we previously possessed 5% of the total market and we now have captured 7% of it, we have grown it by two percentage points. This is strictly a quantitative element, a number.

On the other hand, market development entails more of a qualitative approach. For instance, when we work with our clients in educating them on the use of our product/service we have developed the market. Such development may or may not result to more immediate sales. It probably will in the long run. For the time being, however, we have strengthened the relationship with our client(s) and that's what makes the difference. Such market development takes time and usually follows certain stages. First, we should create awareness about our product or service. Next, we should attempt to create a need or at least a desire about it. Then we should be able to demonstrate benefit to the purchaser; and finally if and when the transaction is consummated we should always try to impress our clients with the "unexpected." At the appropriate future place we will address this as the **Delighters** of an organization.

The specific methodology may include:

- Using existing products, expand to new markets
- Using existing products expand to same markets
- Using new markets with new products
- Using new products with existing markets
- Product modification may be another option

20. New challenges

Every organization is constantly faced with new challenges, both internal and external. Issues like "barriers to entry" "unions" rapid technological discoveries" "change in Governmental regulations" "tariffs and quotas" "changes in the economy" "offshoring" "subsidized companies." All such challenges may prove to be beneficial or harmful to our organization. That will be determined in the future. Currently and from the point of view of designing a Business Plan, it is important that we address these issues. Whether these challenges will be proven to be beneficial or harmful to the organization will depend on the way we address them. We recognize that these challenges are "External" and we don't have much control over them, but if we are positive thinkers, looking at the glass as "half full instead of half empty" we stand a higher chance to overcome them. Let's look at some additional challenges.

21. Industry trends: Can we perform a competitive-trend analysis on the following?

Experts who observe the way an industry acts and reacts could come up with interesting and useful suggestions. Such suggestions are the result of experienced monitoring of the industry and its specific markets. The observations are then "tallied" or "logged" and meaningful conclusions are derived from it. A common way of looking at these observations is through the trend analysis. A trend analysis compares the behavior of an unknown variable in relation to the changes of the known variable. In other words, if we are looking at the number of defects over a period of one month, time is the known factor and the number of defects is the unknown. The two most important types of analyses we deal with are the positive and the negative trend and their degree of strength. This means that we may have a positive and strong or a positive and weak trend. A positive and strong trend means that when the known variable changes, we should be able to predict the behavior-reaction of the unknown variable with a great deal of accuracy. In a weak trend the prediction may not be as accurate. The same holds true for the negative trend. After we perform the trend analysis, we should be ready for the competitive analysis.

A competitive analysis will show us how well we compete in an open market. How well our products/service compare to those of our competitors. These are monitored in relation to exactly that; a picture. The respective graphs which depict the trend analysis are shown in the Appendix-Graph M. Below are some examples of such analyses.

22. Product/service

Here we examine the way the product /service we offer behaves over a period of time. First we look for the kind of slope the trend forms. Is it positive or negative? Then we establish the level of strength. Is it a strong or a weak trend?

If what we observe in the product/service over time increases, then we have a positive trend. If it decreases we then have a negative trend. Based on this, we can then make predictions for future events or actions we wish to take. Once we have determined our own internal conditions through the trend analysis, we then look into the competitiveness of our product/service from two different perspectives. First, how do we compare/compete against our direct competition.

Second, what is our relative position in relation to the industry we are in? Are we competitive? Where do we stand in terms of our competition? Are we at the same level, above or below? What position do we hold in the entire industry?

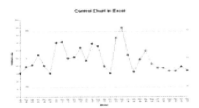   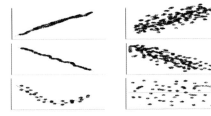

Trend graph A   Trend graph B depicting positive, negative, strong, weak and no-correlation relationships

23. Price

The same holds true about price. The way price behaves over time is significant in determining future pricing decisions and of course profits. Obviously price is one of the five "P's" of Marketing; Product-Place-Price-People-Promotion. Next, we perform our competitive analysis to determine where we stand in terms of our competition and the entire industry. This is an important piece of information that could be incorporated in our advertising campaign and of course in the financial statements. Keep in mind that if the price is too high it might deter people from purchasing the product; the same may occur if the price is too low. It might give the impression of a "cheap" product and again it might turn people off. It's therefore evident that establishing the right price becomes critically important.

24. Image/style/design

All three attributes stated herein, are subject to change and they address both the organization and the product/service. Our company's image will change over time, hopefully in a favorable way. But so will the image of our product/service. Image refers to the impression others have about our company or product. Can we graph it over a period of time? Absolutely. Can we determine the level of competitiveness of our company or product? Of course. The issue then becomes: Once we have determined the trend of our company's image, what do we do with it? Can we use it to make meaningful decisions based on that?

We should. Obviously the same holds true about the style and design of our product/service. However you got to remember one basic rule: *If you don't define your image others will do it for you*.

25. Quality

The level of Quality achieved and maintained in a business is another important factor to observe. Is Quality improving over time? This can easily be answered by performing a trend analysis of it. This analysis may be validated by comparing it to customer returns or complaints or refunds. We should recollect that we have already stated our pledge to Quality in the Executive Summary. Here we look at it from the Marketing's point of view. In other words, how can we capitalize on the level of Quality we produce, whether it's a product or service? Can we incorporate it in the Business Plan and use it as a vehicle to convince bankers or investors that our level of Quality will assure a sustainable business? We should. And once Quality is in place, it's only a matter of presenting it properly in our Business Plan.

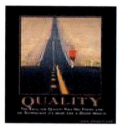

And remember: Your road to QUALITY should always be under construction. Quality is NOT a destination but an endless journey

26. Perceived value

A philosopher once said: *People don't act according to reality, but in accordance to their perception of reality.* It's ironic that we are addressing reality and at the same time we propose that reality is a mere perception. This isn't an irony, it's an oxymoron. However a very true oxymoron. Why? Because that's how human nature works. An example of this may be the behavior of students as a result of their perception of a professor. If students believe (perceive) that the professor is tough and demanding they may avoid registering for her/his class, simply because of a perception. When in reality such perception may not be true. Therefore the issue is: What type of impression do we cultivate and convey about our organization? And that's an issue that should be addressed in our Business Plan.

27. Brand recognition

A brand is a name, a phrase, a design, a symbol or even a combination of all of these to identify a product/service and distinguish it from those of the competitors. Along with the "brand name" comes brand loyalty, brand licensing, brand equity and brand personality. The issue that we are examining here is twofold: First, can our brand be competitive? And second, how could a trend

people's responses on a chart, to determine viability of our brand. Keep in mind, that it takes forever to build a positive brand name, but it takes "the blink of an eye" to destroy it or lose it.
As it was stated above about image, it's even more crucial that we clearly define our brand, because if we don't others will do it for us. If you ask what's wrong with that? Well, others don't know our company or products as well as we do. Therefore there is a possibility to "brand" us wrongly. That's why it's imperative that **we** go through the branding process; **we** establish it.

28. Customer relationships

Very seldom a company will have a customer who doesn't purchase anything from its competitors. For various reasons, many of our customers buy from our competitors. This is a fact. The question becomes: How can we ensure that the association we have with our customers is continuously strengthened? What can we do to make certain that the product/service we provide is superior to that of our competitors? The CSIPO model may come handy. In addition we should realize and internalize that:

a) Service improperly performed can't be recalled
b) Excellent service is produced at time of delivery; service can't be produced in advance
c) The "service" can't be demonstrated or sent to the customer as a sample

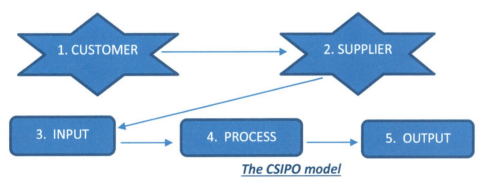

The CSIPO model

The steps of CSIPO are numbered. We begin with the customer's request, then we go to the supplier stating: *Dear supplier, my direct customer, who is your indirect customer, wants specs a, b, c. How can you best serve me so I can service my customer in the best way possible? Of course the IPO (Input-Process-Output) is self-explanatory and common to any organization.*

Once we understand these basic principles and do something about them, we could argue that our product/service is competitive. It's imperative that the competitiveness is stated by the customer, not just by us. We may think we are competitive; but does it matter what we think, if our customers don't feel the same? Of course not. In closing, it's imperative that we become and remain competitive in the eye of the customer and also track such competitiveness via a trend analysis.

29. Delivery time of product/service

When an organization buys a product or service, is delivery time important? If yes, why? Well, let's examine the scenario where a retail company that sells cloths places an order for the next season's supplies to a vendor whose factory is overseas. The merchandise is expected to arrive in July to be distributed by August 1st so the retailer could capture the autumn season. That's all planned and scheduled to arrive on time. For unforeseen reasons the delivery is delayed by three weeks. Can you realize the detrimental impact this may have on to the retailer?

Here is another example. A restaurant wishes to have its daily deliveries between 9:00 and 11:00 a.m. The reason is that during this two-hour window the place has already finished serving breakfast and is preparing for lunch. If the deliveries of meat, produce, paper supplies, etc. is done during the 9:00 to 11:00am window the restaurateur has ample time to receive the goods, check the delivery for accuracy and store them accordingly. On the other hand, if the truck with all these supplies arrives at 12:30 p.m., when the restaurant is excessively busy serving lunch, the restaurateur isn't happy and most likely will turn the delivery away, thus creating a discontent and higher costs.

Now, if we were the delivery company, do we realize the importance of proper timing? We should….. In addition, can we track the times of our deliveries and determine if they comply with customer requests? Obviously we could. A trend analysis combined with statistical control, could be very helpful. The trend analysis could tell us how we are performing over time and the SPC can tell us how close we are to the unacceptable times; i.e. Upper and Lower Control Limits (UCL-LCL) The graph below explains the issue.

30. **Convenience of use**

One of the reasons people buy a product/service is to make their lives easier. Therefore it's our responsibility to make the use of it as "user friendly" as we possibly can. In doing so, we should look into the "competitiveness" of use. How competitive are we? What's the industry doing? What's the competition doing about it? How do our customers feel about the benefit our product/service offers in relation to the competition? Can we compile this information? We trust we can. Once we compile it, can we use the appropriate tools to see if there is a trend? Could it be that the "convenience of use" is declining? Of course it could. And such decline may not necessarily be our fault. It could easily be that the competitors' products are more user friendly and the customers, subconsciously and unintentionally may be rating our product as an inferior one. We will not know that, unless we track our customers' feelings-impressions and reflect them on a chart, thus performing a trend analysis.

31. **Credit policies**

Business is all about credit; very seldom we see cash transactions especially with big corporations. Therefore credit policies and procedures become an important element to a business. One could claim that "Credit Policies" is a financial issue; and that's correct. However, credit terms could influence sales and marketing in general, therefore we address it here. Keep in mind that the intent of this document is NOT to present an academic textbook that will be critiqued and evaluated by other academicians. All we are trying to accomplish here is to provide a blueprint to a well-designed Business Plan.

So speaking of credit terms here are some common expressions: Net 30, or 5/15-Net 60, or 2% discount for immediate payment. Today we see this with gasoline stations; cash price at the pump may be 5 cents lower than the credit price. What we need to look into is what our customers like or prefer. In addition we need to determine what our competition is doing about it? What terms do they provide to their customers? Are our customers interested in their credit terms? Do they find our credit terms sufficient or superior? What else can we do to please our customers? Are the credit terms the only issues our customers are concerned with? Can we provide quantity discounts? Can we track all this? We should….. In addition can we perform a trend analysis to see how our credit terms are changing over time? Which direction are they going? We should; actually we have an obligation to do so. Here we need to clarify one issue: We don't imply that we should be following our competitors and do as they do. What we are saying is that we should be aware of what they are doing. Then we should initiate our actions/tactics that are beneficial to our clients and of course to the organization.

32. *Customer/client service*

We have found out that with many of our clients, price is a secondary issue. Many of them are more interested in the quality of service we provide. More specifically our customer may value reliability and consistency higher than cost. They don't mind if they have to pay an extra 2% as long as they can be assured of issues like consistency, accuracy and reliability.
Once we understand the significance of these issues, we should look into our competitors. What are they doing about these issues? Are they addressing them? If so how? Then we should be able to determine our competitiveness. In addition, we should look at the whole industry and determine where do we stand in it?

33. *Social consciousness*

We all know how ruthless competition is. Companies will try anything under the radar to convince customers to go to them. Customers however, have become more and more knowledgeable about these techniques. As a matter of fact, we have found out that customers, in general, have their ways of evaluating companies. They look into different factors, one of which is the social responsibility of a business. A socially responsible organization realizes that it is part of a larger society and that is accountable to that society for its actions. How socially conscientious are we? Do we fulfill our social responsibility and if so to what extend?
Customers compare companies based on that. Therefore it becomes imperative that
a) we are socially conscious and
b) we do it better than our competitors
Given that, we should continuously try to improve, tracking our social responsibility throughout the years becomes a "must." Of course this can easily be accomplished through the use of histograms or a trend analysis.

34. *Product mix/line*

Most companies categorize their products/services by product line and then they classify them by product mix. A product line refers to a group of related products that satisfy a class of needs that are used together and are sold to the same customer group.

A product mix refers to the number of product lines offered by the company.

Do we have product lines and product mix in our organization? If so, how does it compare to those of our competitors? Can we run this comparative analysis to determine how competitive we are? We should. In running this comparison could we use a trend analysis? How would we use it? By tracking how our product lines and the specific products within them behave over time. If we are interested in finding out how the product/service is performing, could we track the daily or the weekly sales to determine if there is a trend? That's easy. All we need to do is record the sales-historical data and then a trend will be shown.

35. *Projected market share and market growth*

Market share and growth are two critical factors that any business should monitor to determine how they are behaving over time. Obviously we aren't the only seller in the industry. Unless we are talking about a monopoly, we have several sellers, some of whom are our competitors. Could we observe what our competitors do in this respect and compare our performance to theirs? I guess we could. Here we monitor our market growth. How is it reacting over time? In other words, if we compiled data about our market share last year and we do the same this year, could we determine if there was a change? And if so, what type, an increase or a decrease. This way we could identify how our company does and then make decisions about future activities.

As in most previous cases, a trend analysis may be useful.

36. *Operational efficiency, effectiveness and productivity*

If we were able to determine the level of efficiency, effectiveness and productivity we operate under and compare them to the industry and our competitors, we should be in a very strong comparative position. These characteristics contribute immensely towards our organization's success. All three are critical factors that add value to our organization. Do we know their "values?"

In other words, how efficient are we? What is our rate of effectiveness along with our productivity ratio? Is it important that we know that? Why? Do we have any idea how our competitors are doing in reference to these attributes? Should we know that? Of course. Why? Because knowing how these three attributes compare to our competitors, it could help us in a number of areas; like pricing, discounts offering, incentives we offer to our people and so many other things we can do with it.

37. *Operational costs (high-medium-low)*

Running a business costs money. Such costs play an important role in a number of areas. Calculation of net income, contribution margin, product cost, selling price etc.
Operational costs could be relatively low, medium or high. The issue we are examining here is: How do our operational costs compare to the industry and those of our competitors? If we are lower than our competition, we have room for certain action(s). If we are higher, chances are that we may not be as competitive. Therefore it's important that we know:
a) type and height of costs
b) how they compare to our competitors
c) how we compare to the industry we are in; and all that should be reflected in our Plan. In determining such costs we should be conservatively pessimistic.

38. *Technological competence - IT / Web*

One of the greatest and important resources in any business is technology. Possessing state-of-the-art technology is one thing, having knowledgeable people to work with it effectively and efficiently, is another. Satisfying the first part of our premise is easy, having people who possess the skills and are constantly trained on new technological programs is the harder of the two. Do we own advanced technological equipment that our people don't know how to use? Obviously our competitors look into these concerns too. The issue becomes, how do we compare to them? Is our web site working for us or against us?

39. *Patents/trademarks/copyrights*

All organizations show the value of their current and fixed assets in a balance sheet. They are called "tangibles." There is another category of assets, that of "intangibles" that not many organizations are qualifying to enlist in their balance sheet.
Such assets are Patents, Trademarks, Goodwill and Copyrights. Do we own any?
Does our competition own any? If they don't and let's say that we have our own patents; does that give us a competitive advantage? Of course it does and that's why we suggest that such intangible assets should be shown in our Business Plan.

40. *Creative/innovative ability*

Creativity: The ability to produce something new through imaginative skill, whether it is a new solution to a problem, a new method, a new device, or a new artistic object or form that has value or usefulness. Put simply, Creativity means we design and produce something original, make something for the first time.

41. Innovation

Innovation involves deliberate application of information, imagination, and initiative in deriving greater or different value from resources. It encompasses all processes by which new ideas are generated and converted into useful products or services.

In business, to claim that we came up with an innovation, the idea must be replicable at an economical cost and should satisfy a specific need. In a social context, innovation is equally important in devising new collaborative methods.

Now that we have an idea of creativity and innovation, we need to examine how creative and innovate are we? When was the last time we used either one or both to enhance our processes? We have an obligation to do that just like we have a responsibility to track our competitors' creative and innovative ability and progress.

42. SWOT or SCOT analysis

A SWOT analysis addresses Strengths-Weaknesses-Opportunities-Threats. We prefer the SCOT where the "C" stands for challenges. The word "Weaknesses" entails more of a negative connotation where "challenges" gives to it a different view, that of a positive thinker. All businesses are affected by all four factors in some way, positively or negatively. The chart that follows, which has also been submitted as an exhibit, clearly demonstrates the meaning and intent of the form. Unlike most users/presenters of the SWOT analysis, where they use a square divided in four sub-squares, we have developed a more user friendly and effective SWOT form.

In applying the form one needs to understand the meaning of the "Internal" and "external" environment and the way they relate to strengths/weaknesses and opportunities/threats respectively. More specifically, strengths and weaknesses are listed under the "internal" environment. This means that strengths and weaknesses could be controlled and managed by the company, while opportunities and threats can't be controlled and managed by the company. On the contrary, being external forces we enlist them in the SWOT form and monitor its influence on to the firm. Examples of each category are given below.

<u>Strengths</u>: Resources, financial reserves, market share, processes, people, location
<u>Weaknesses</u>: Poor reputation, inadequate cash-flow, lack of competitiveness
<u>Opportunities</u>: Economic factors-interest rate, global influences, export-import trade
<u>Threats</u>: Political effects, legislation, IT developments, seasonality and weather effects
Next you have the form we have designed for the implementation of the SWOT analysis.

When you look at the form, pay attention to the "ranking" columns. We present an unusual approach. The purpose of it is to rate the four areas and at a later time, say six months, we should go back and reexamine-reevaluate our company in these four areas. By doing that we could determine the direction our organization is going.

INTERNAL ENVIRONMENT				EXTERNAL ENVIRONMENT			
STRENGTHS (1)	Rank (2)	Rank (3)	WEAKNESSES (4)	OPPORTUNITIES (5)	Rank (6)	Rank (7)	THREATS (8)

INSTRUCTIONS: Identify some strong points-qualities you have (personal or organizational) and list them in the "STRENGTHS" column; then "Rank" them in column (2) on a scale 1-10, with 10 being the highest score. Do the same for what you consider to be your weak points. List them under "WEAKNESSES" and rank them accordingly, in column (3). Do the same for the rest of the form. Six months later go back and reassess your initial findings. You can then determine the areas and the degree of change-improvement.

Competitive Analysis

On a scale 1-10 with 10 being the highest, evaluate the attributes below

ATRIBUTES	Our Strengths	The Industry	Competitor #1	Competitor #2	Competitor #3	Value to client	Comments
Products							
Service							
Confidence							
Quality							
Price							
Selection							
Consistency							
Reliability							
Stability							
Trust							
Expertise							
Reputation							
Exec. Team							
Appearance							
Sales Method							
Credit Policies							
Advertising							
P R, Publicity							
Image/Appearance							
Location							
Distribution							
Financial stability							
Training							
Patents/Trademarks							

NOTES

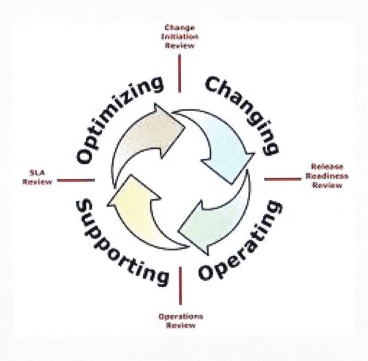

OPERATIONAL CONSIDERATIONS

Introduction

The next major area our Business Plan should address is the organization's Operational considerations. Basically there are three major areas that directly affect the Operations.

1. **People**
2. **Capital Equipment**
3. **Processes/Operations**

We shall address all three in detail.

43.   1. People

This topic will be divided into:

A)   Management
B)   Personnel

A. Management: As Management we understand any and all Directors of the business; people who have subordinates.

How many types and levels of Management should we have?

For instance, should we have:

→ A Board of Directors

→ An Executive Board

→ An Executive Committee, like president, Senior VP's, VP's, Regional Directors etc.

→ A Committee of Overseers

→ A National/International Advisory Board

→ Management Teams

For each group of Management identified above we should determine how many people will we have in each? Do we want a Board of Directors consisted of five Board Members only or should we have 20?

The same should hold true with all the groups mentioned above.

Once we determine the number of individuals we should have in each, we should next define the credentials they should have in order to qualify for the position. In the job description we should also define the educational requirements.

Duties and responsibilities of each member should also be defined.

The same should be true for their salaries. Regarding the salaries we should make sure that they are reflected in the Income Statement accordingly. In addition, the Managers' background should be presented in the Business Plan. Especially if we have certain members who are regarded highly in the eyes of the public, thus they add prestige to the company, we should highlight such a background.

If these people have letters of recommendation from previous engagements, we should list them in here, too.

If any of these people are investing any money in the business, it should also be demonstrated in the Business Plan. This way we strengthen our position, because we demonstrate our seriousness and commitment to the project.

Finally we should list the years of business experience Management has in this field.

B) Personnel

Most of the questions that were asked about Management should apply to the selection of our Personnel. By incorporating in our Business Plan the process and the criteria we followed in the selection of our Personnel, we appear professional and convincing. Such criteria should include some or more of the following.

1. How many full-time versus part-time employees should we have?
2. What type of benefits should we offer to our people?
3. What type of training should we make available to our employees?
4. What would be the span of control?
5. Their level of experience in the business we are in?

Finally we should also give a statement explaining why and how we are going to succeed.

44. Capital Equipment (also called Fixed Assets)

The four main areas that should be addressed here are:

A) Buildings and Land
B) Machinery and Equipment
C) Office Furniture
D) Intangible assets, i.e. Trademarks, copyrights, goodwill etc.

With all four categories we should ask and address the following questions:

1. What type of fixed assets do we need?
2. When do we need them? Obviously not everything will be needed on day one.
3. How are we going to pay for them?
4. Are we going to purchase them or lease them?
5. What depreciation methods are we going to use?
6. What intangible assets do we bring into the business, if any

45. Procedures/Operations

As starters we should identify all Procedures and Operations performed in our business. Under "Procedures" we should identify all the systems, subsystems, methods and practices we use in our business and standardize them.

For all major procedures we should develop manuals and such manuals should be referenced in our Business Plan.

In terms of "Operations" first we should classify them into

*Strategic

*Tactical

*Operational or front line

Once we establish such classification we should then move into identifying and outlining the specific functions that should take place in each level.

As noted with Procedures, an Operations manual should be designed and standardized. Such an Operations manual should be referenced in our Business Plan as well.

46. Engineers and R&D

Do we have engineers in our organization? How many? What are their areas of expertise and involvement? How many of them are engaged in R&D? What have been their innovations or developments? Is there an R&D budget? What is the annual cost of the R&D department? Is there a correlation between the R&D department and the Innovation & Creativity department? Do we have an Innovation & Creativity department? If so, what type of Innovations have we instituted recently? If not, are we working on any? These are some of the questions potential investors will raise and have interest in. The equitable answer to these concerns will greatly determine the way potential investors look at our organization.

47. Benchmarking, ISO series

Benchmarking is the process of comparing one's business processes and performance metrics to industry bests and/or best practices from other industries. Dimensions typically measured are quality, reliability, consistency, customer/employee satisfaction and cost. On page 40 we have provided an "Attributes Grid" that could be instrumental at this point. During benchmarking, management identifies the best firms in the industry, or in a similar industry, and compares the results and processes of those studied to one's own results and processes. This way, they learn how well the targets perform and more importantly, the business processes that explain why these firms are successful. Are we benchmarking our company? If so, what's the deviation from the benchmark? Have we reached the level where other organizations are using us as a benchmark? Could we? These are some genuine concerns that should be addressed in our analysis.

In terms of ISO first, we need to understand what ISO is. It's a set of standards, procedures and guidelines for quality in the manufacturing and service industries from the International Organization for Standardization. There are several such ISO standards. The way we should address this should be: Are we ISO certified? If not, could we be? What's the benefit from such certification? How do our customers view ISO certification? Keep in mind, that in many European transactions, some companies won't even talk to you unless you are ISO certified. This notion has been gaining ground in the US since the early 90's. In conclusion, if we are ISO certified we should demonstrate it in the business plan. If we are in the process of being certified, we should also state it. If we aren't, skip the topic totally.

48. Learning curve

In short, the Learning Curve concept represents efficiencies gained from experience. We should track these efficiencies and reflect them on to our business plan. This way we demonstrate to our potential investors and customers that we are concerned with the level of efficiency, effectiveness and productivity presented earlier. This makes us look good in the general public's eyes. It creates a favorable image about our organization.

49. People, training / development

Our Business Plan should address the issue of Continuous Improvement along with the recognition that our Human Resource capital is not just another asset, but the most valuable element of our business. Demonstrating that we value our employees and their innovative ideas makes our organization more appealing to the general public. Here we have the opportunity to showcase our beliefs about training and employee development.

How much out of our total budget is appropriated to training, to employee growth and development? How frequently do we send our employees to training? How frequently do we bring in experts to train our people? Can we document this? If yes, we should incorporate it into our business plan.

Finally we should be able to show how many of our employees are full-time vs. part-time employees and their qualifications. In addition, we should demonstrate that we don't discriminate against part-time employees. If they want to be sent to training we do so. The reason for this is the following: People and specifically customers don't know, nor do they care, if an employee is full or part-time. What they see is a person who serves them at the time and that person represents the company. If the company's philosophy is: Well this person-employee is a part-time employee, therefore I don't have to invest into her/his training, constitutes a deadly mistake.

To better understand this take the scenario of a university that has full-time and part-time professors. Do the students care if the professor is a pert-timer? Of course not. What the students (customers) want is a qualified professor who can teach them effectively. Therefore, if the university says: The part-time professors will not be sent to a faculty retreat, actually it is causing self-inflicted injuries.

50. Risks

This issue is so important that we have devoted a major segment to it. However, at this point we need to examine how competitive we are in terms of risks and their impact to our business. We should be able to identify all or at least most risks concerning our business. Yes, there are unpredictable events that might entail some risk but nevertheless, we should have a mechanism in place to predict most of them. As it was stated above, we will fully explore this at the appropriate segment, but here we ought to look at risks as they compare to those of our competitors. Additionally, we should look into methodologies of keeping track of all risks and the way we dealt with them. A trend analysis, check-sheet, or a histogram may be excellent tools in tracing how risks behave over time.

51. QC tools

Just like accountants, carpenters, dentists, plumbers and builders work with a variety of tools, business professionals do the same. Some of the most commonly known tools are the so called "graphs" and as business professionals we have a plethora of them. Below, we have a list and a pictorial representation of some of them. Make sure that we use as many as we possibly can in our business plan. Remember, a picture is worth a thousand words.

The one thing that makes us different from our competition is that instead of having Quality Control People (QCP) we have all of our employees act as QCP. The reason for this is our unique and innovative belief about Quality. We feel that every person in our organization knows the level of Quality that s/he should be performing at and they are responsible for delivering the desired Quality. Therefore we don't need any QCP. That should be highlighted in our Business Plan, because it underlines out commitment to Quality.

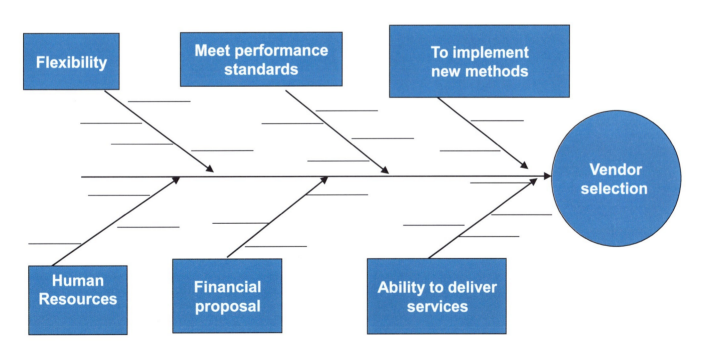

FISH-BONE DIAGRAM aka CAUSE-AND-EFFECT DIAGRAM

More diagrams and charts in the Appendix

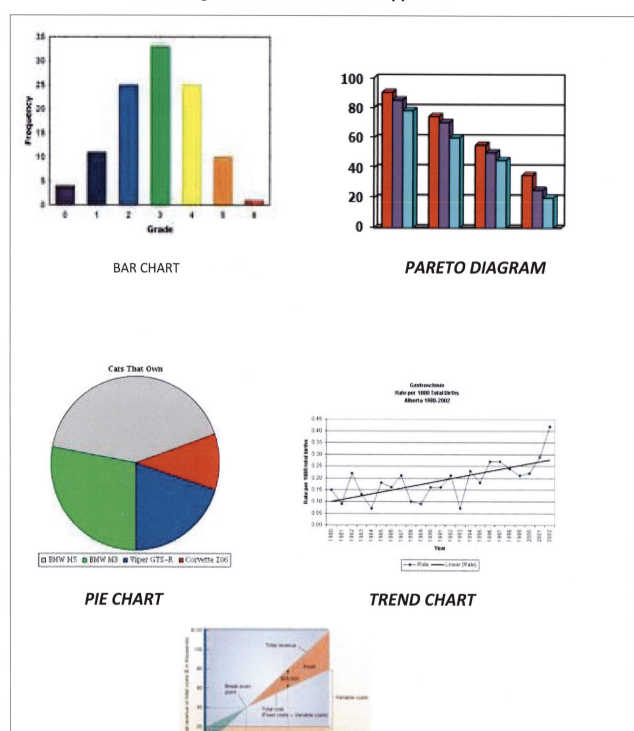

52. Top-down/Bottom-up approach and Tall /Flat hierarchy

A structural and organizational appearance is important to any business plan. The way information and delegation flows is also important. There are two basic approaches: The Top-Down and the Bottom-up. The Top-Down implies more of an authoritarian business environment, while the Bottom-up allows for more participation by the lower level personnel.

As part of this organizational structure or flow of information, we should also examine the specific organizational hierarchy. Again, we have two different and distinct approaches; the Tall versus the Flat model. In the first, we use countless (20-30) levels of management. Where in the later, the hierarchical levels are 4-5. Both have their place and the respective advantages and disadvantages. What we should be concerned with is, whatever structural or hierarchical approach takes place in our business, we should declare it, and demonstrate why it's best to do it this way.

Flat Hierarchy with 3 management levels

Tall Hierarchy with 10 levels of management

53. Layout considerations

Facility layout has to do with the arrangement of workstations, equipment and machinery. It directly influences efficiency, effectiveness, productivity and ROI. The purpose of the company layout and the business plan is for us to demonstrate that we intentionally have chosen the respective layout, which is an efficient way of running our business. In many businesses we have seen redundant work and movement. By addressing the layout issue, we are assuring the public that we are concerned with efficiency and we show it.

54. Location concerns

We have all heard the expression "the three most important factors contributing to the success of a business are: Location-Location-Location." Determining the proper location is vitally important. Whether we are referring to a "storefront" or an office area or even a warehouse, the equitable location could influence your potential investors or public favorably. Show how our organization benefits from the use of the current or the selected location. Keep in mind that for storage location selection we have scientific methods like the center-of-gravity method, or the location-break-even-analysis, proximity to markets, or proximity to suppliers. To determine which method to use we look into factors like cost of labor, cost of land, cost of transportation, and closeness to market and competitors.

So, all we are saying here is, address the location issue and present it accordingly.

55. Team building and self-directed teams

First we need to understand what team means. We like the acronym that says:

T-ogether

E-veryone

A-chieves

M-ore.

Next, we should realize that the TEAM effort is greater than the sum of the individual participants' strengths; that's why we say when we adopt the TEAM mentality 2+2=5.

Additionally in our business plan we should include things like:

Team composition (who is in what team and why; if we have a world renowned personality in one of our teams we should demonstrate it. Here we don't mean a listing of all teams; just the most influential ones.)

Next we should demonstrate how we assure Team effectiveness and Team-Building skills.

Finally we should explain why we believe in the Team mentality avoiding the "group" approach. Exhibiting all this in our business plan, the reader of it should feel comfortable with the potentiality of success of our business

56. Core competencies

We have covered the SWOT analysis previously. In this segment we don't only show our strengths, but we clearly demonstrate what we are proficient in. What are the areas of expertise and undeniable capabilities? Is it "product quality" or "reliability" or "consistency?" Whatever our core competency or competencies are, we "display" them here. In other words, we tell the world why and how <u>we are the best</u> and why they should be doing business with us. In doing so, we need to be tactful so we won't sound egotistical or arrogant. In referring to our competencies we should list 3-4 of them only. Yes, we perform many different functions well and we could demonstrate competence in all of them. However, if we say that we are experts in everything we do, we run the risk to lose believability and trust. Next we address "Outsourcing" which is one of the ways to solidify what we stated above. In other words, yes we have several core competencies, but we outsource some functions because others perform them better than we do.

57. Outsourcing

The function of outsourcing has been misunderstood or misrepresented by some. Generally speaking outsourcing is the contracting out to an external provider a function previously performed in-house. In this sense, two organizations may enter into a contractual agreement involving an exchange of services and payments. For the record, in recent years outsourcing has been associated with offshore outsourcing.

Additionally, terms like extended organizational networks, or near-shoring, or multi-sourcing have been used to demonstrate various forms of outsourcing.

Some view outsourcing negatively, and rightfully so, because it doesn't come without any drawbacks or shortcomings. However, if we are positive thinkers, and we look at the glass as half full instead of half empty, we could identify more benefits than disadvantages.

If we are outsourcing, our Business Plan should depict that, and it should cite the reasons why we do it. Such reasons for outsourcing could be:

a) Cost savings and restructuring, which gives us operational leverage
b) Allows us to "Focus on Core Business" or what we do best
c) Improved Quality
d) Utilization of better and larger talent
e) Benefit from their knowledge and expertise
f) We free-up capacity for the production of other items
g) Most likely reduces time to market
h) Possibly provides tax advantages
i) Minimizes risk, especially if we use multiple sources
j) We are exposed to others work ethics
k) Become acquainted with other cultures, even with domestic outsourcing

If we are able to incorporate some/most of these benefits into our business plan, it will have a much higher probability of being viewed favorably by the public.

When something has advantages it's expected to also have potential Disadvantages and possibly Risks.

- Overall loss or reduction of control

- External risks
  - Geopolitical Instability, is we are outsourcing off-shore
  - Security, privacy, and intellectual property loss
  - Vendor take-over by a competitor along with inadequate vendor capabilities
- Internal risk
  - Failure to create joint venture
  - Possible higher costs especially "legal"
  - Faced with unrealistic expectations
  - Lack of organizational preparedness
  - Outsourcing management overhead
- Negative staff impact
  - Staff loss or turnover
  - Knowledge loss to another organization
  - Loss of team spirit and development of fear for job loss
- Personal impact on career, lifestyle and reputation

58. Groupthink vs Brainstorming

All we will attempt to do here is clarify the difference between "Groupthink" and "Brain-storming." Brainstorming is a technique for generating new ideas, whereas in Groupthink we are looking for unanimity on the idea. The picture below demonstrates that. Under brainstorming, we have people come up with ideas that we post on a board and then we select the appealing ones. In Groupthink people don't "conclude" until a unanimous solution is reached. As it's shown in the Groupthink picture, the group members are celebrating their effort.

Brainstorming   *Groupthink*

Why do we address this issue? Because it will be nice to include in our Business Plan that during our R&D for new products we deploy techniques like these two. That's all......

59. Conflict resolution

Are organizations faced with conflict? All the time. Do we have "conflict" in our company? Of course we do. Why are we mentioning this issue as part of our business plan? Because it is only appropriate to demonstrate that we are aware of the fact that conflict exists and we have devised methodologies to deal with it. It makes us look proactive and it creates a favorable image about the way we run our business, which strengthens people's beliefs and confidence in us. We also suggest that we enlist some of the techniques we usually deploy to resolve conflict. Some of the most effective have been:

- Problem Depersonalization
- The Sandwich technique
- The Triangle technique

60. Capacity concerns

Capacity is defined as the ability to hold, to contain, to accommodate or to process over a period of time. The amount and level of capacity an organization operates under is significant to its success. Underutilized capacity means low ROI. On the other hand, inadequate capacity means business lost, thus opportunity lost, thus lower profit. Once we understand this basic premise, we can then move on to the types of capacity like: Minimum, maximum, average, theoretical, realistic and attainable, are some of the terms used in business.

Obviously the intent here isn't to teach you the role and effect of capacity; rather the scope is to convince you that we should incorporate our capacity situation and its specifics into our Business Plan. By doing that we demonstrate to the public that we are aware of what is happening in terms of capacity and that we attempt to optimize it at all times. This way the public is now convinced that we have enhanced our probability for success. A chart indicating what level of capacity we were operating under, say three years ago, and another depicting what level of capacity we are operating under now (assuming that now we have higher utilization of our capacity) will make our company look very competitive.

In our attempt to demonstrate the level of capacity we operate under, we should also address the effect of marginal increase of capacity. In other words, we should demonstrate the level of production at which the capacity will have to increase. Identifying that level of production and operating at or just below it, we prove to the public that we are operating a highly efficient

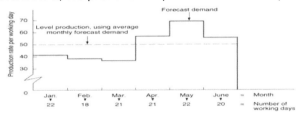

organization.

61. Machinery and Equipment

This item is directly related to capacity analyzed above. With some business plans we have seen it addressed concurrently. What we are talking about here is: First, comprise a list of all of our tools, machinery, equipment and even processing supplies. Next, maintain a clear, accurate and updated log of each. For instance, lease contract, purchase value, cost, depreciation, maintenance, upgrades, type of work performed by each, life expectancy, and remaining potential productive output. By maintaining this information and including it in our Business Plan, we give the impression that our organization is professional, well organized, and efficient. These are attributes that are viewed very favorably by the public. Finally, we comprise a value list of all machinery and equipment. This list with dollar values strengthens our Business Plan because we have an opportunity to show the value of these assets at a point unrelated to the evaluation of the business.

62. Logistics, Supply-Chain Management

Supply chain management (SCM) refers to the efficient transmission and oversight of materials, information, and finances as they move in a process from supplier to manufacturer, to wholesaler, to intermediaries, to retailer to consumer or customer. Supply chain management involves coordinating and integrating these flows both within and among companies. It is said that the ultimate goal of any effective supply chain management system is to reduce waste and all non-value added activities. JIT may come very handy.

Logistics is the management of the flow of goods and services between the point of origin and the point of utilization, in order to meet the requirements of customers.

Logistics involves the integration of information, transportation, inventory, warehousing, material handling, and packaging, and often security. Logistics is a channel of the supply chain which adds the value of time and place utility. Today the complexity of production logistics can be modeled, analyzed, visualized and optimized by various simulation software packages.

Third party logistics is also addressed by SCM.
How does all this come into play with what we are discussing under "Business Plan?" The answer is rather obvious. By addressing the issue of SCM and Logistics we demonstrate to the public that we are an efficiently operating organization.

LOGISTICS AND SUPPLY-CHAIN-MANAGEMENT GRAPH

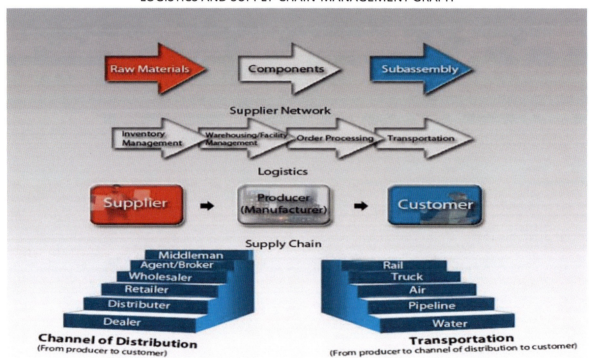

63. Policies, Procedures and Manuals

Just like the marketing eras we discussed in the beginning of this book, policies, procedures and manuals have gone their path as well. As the size of an organization increases, so does the need for these three "tools." In a utopia world none of the three would be required. Unfortunately, we are living in a world where the law suits have become part of life and people's work ethics aren't at the highest possible point. Therefore in an attempt to avoid or minimize any negative impact, organizations had to develop policies, procedures and manuals. Do we have policies, procedures and manuals in our company? Of course we do. Then let's demonstrate in our business plan the type and kind of policies, procedures and manuals we have. It will definitely create a positive image to the public.

64. Forecasting

Forecasting is the process of making predictive statements about events whose actual outcomes (typically) have not yet occurred. A common place example might be estimation for some variable of interest at some specified future date. Prediction or estimation are also terms used in place of forecasting, but are more general terms. Both might refer to formal statistical methods employing time series, cross-sectional data, or alternatively to less formal judgmental methods.
Risk and uncertainty are central to forecasting and prediction; it is generally considered good practice to indicate the degree of uncertainty attaching to forecasts. Forecasting is used in the practice of Customer Demand Planning in every-day business forecasting for all types of companies, manufacturing, merchandizing or service. The discipline of demand planning, also known as supply chain forecasting, embraces both statistical forecasting and a consensus process. An important, although often ignored aspect of forecasting, is the relationship it holds with planning. Forecasting can be described as predicting what the future *will* look like, whereas planning predicts what the future *should* look like. The forecasting methods may be classified in many different categories. The most common may be: Quantitative and Qualitative. There is no single right forecasting method to use for all companies and in all situations. Selection of a method should be based on our objectives, conditions and purpose we want to achieve, at any given time. Under the Quantitative category we have what is known as Time Series Methods. Such methods use historical data as the basis of estimating future outcomes. Methods like a) The Moving Averages, b) Weighted Moving Averages, c) Exponential Smoothing, d) Regression Analysis, e) Coefficient of Correlation or Determination may be the most common; while on the Qualitative side or otherwise called the Judgmental methods we have: a) The Delphi Technique, b) People's estimates, c) Surveys, d) Questionnaires to mention a few.

A business plan that incorporates forecasting techniques, both Quantitative and Qualitative, is far more convincing. It demonstrates that the budgeted data that we incorporated in our budgets have been calculated scientifically, thus they are truthful and believable.

65. MRP and CRP

MRP and CRP stand for Material Requirements Planning and Capacity Requirements Planning, respectively. MRP deploys depended demand techniques, Bill of Materials, Inventory, customer orders and Master Production Schedule to determine material requirements. Every well-organized business should perform these two major functions, religiously. As a matter of fact, the industry has developed highly sophisticated computerized systems on both. Planning the materials needed in a production or service environment, is not easy. Especially with large size companies such processes tend to become cumbersome, highly complex and lengthy. An MRP system simplifies the entire process, making inventory and materials decisions easy to reach and follow. Additionally, an MRP system will support the JIT and Supply Chain Management philosophy explained previously. With

MRP you have the right quantities, at the right place and at the right time, thus minimizing or possibly eliminating waste. When waste is eliminated, ROI improves; a highly desired outcome for any business.

Alongside with MRP comes the Planning of Capacity. Basically, once we determine what is needed, at what place and time, we can then plan for the appropriate capacity, i.e. space, machinery, equipment, HR, tools and the alike. This way we avoid any shortage or excess in capacity, thus achieving the highest ROI for it.

Well, if both functions aim at improving ROI don't you think that potential investors and customers would love it? We know they would. That's why we suggest that every Business Plan should incorporate MRP and CRP methodologies.

66. *Scheduling: Forward-Backward*

In the immediately preceding topic we covered MRP and CRP. Both address PLANNING. Now that we managed the overall planning, we should get "down to the specifics." This is addressed in the scheduling. Planning the overall production for the next six months is accomplished via MRP. What should and will be produced, in what specific quantities, on a daily or even hourly basis, is regulated via scheduling. Scheduling is usually done in its "forward" mode but it could also be executed in what the industry calls "backward" mode. In the forward we schedule production jobs start as soon as the job requirements are known. Where backward scheduling begins with the due date and schedules the last operation first and the other job steps in reverse order. Here we may want to recollect the "Push vs. Pull" system.

Push=forward scheduling;

Pull=backward scheduling.

Another significant factor that plays an important role on scheduling is the way we prioritize the execution of the multiple jobs we have. Obviously business professionals have developed techniques like the earliest due date, or the shorted time required or the least operations required or even the factor assignment method. Regardless of how scheduling is performed, make sure that we incorporate it in our Business Plan.

NOTES

Financial Considerations

FINANCIAL REQUIREMENTS

In most cases we write a Business Plan because we need funding for an existing business or for a new start-up. Therefore the first thing we should state is:

a) How much funding is needed?
b) For what purpose?
c) In what intervals?
d) How and when will it be paid back and with what ROI?

Next we need to differentiate between existing businesses and start-ups. With an existing business we have historical data to base our projections on; a fairly easy task. However with a new business the compilation of financial statements and their projection isn't an easy task. Data from the industry and from our competition may be helpful.

67. Overview of Financial statements and projections

Every well organized and presented Business Plan should include accurate, detailed, updated, correct and convincing financial information. Whether we have an existing business or a start-up, the responsibility remains the same. Such information should include most of the following:

67-a) - Basic financial statements (Balance Sheet, Income Statement, Cash-Flow, Retained Earnings)

Balance Sheet (s)

For an existing business provide the past three years Balance Sheets, current Balance Sheet up-to-date, and then the projected for next year

For a start-up comprise the Balance Sheet based on well calculated projections, forecasts and estimates

Income Statement

For an existing business, same as above. The projected Income Statements should be monthly for the first year and quarterly for years two and beyond

Cash-Flow

Same as above

Retained Earnings

Same as above

> **A word of advice:** With the statements stated above be consciously pessimistic; when in doubt go with the conservative amount.

67-b) - A ratio analysis including at least 10-12 vitally important ratios (for existing entities)

Liquidity ratios

-Current ratios

-Acid-Test ratios

Leverage (debt) ratios

-Debt ratios

-Interest coverage

Profitability ratios

-Gross margin ratios

-Net margin ratios

-Return on assets

-Return on equity

-Earnings per share

Activity ratios

-Average collection period

-Inventory turnover

-Fixed asset turnover

-Total asset turnover

67-c) - An Owner's Equity statement

Here we should demonstrate how the owner's equity will be affected in the next five years by the retained earnings or other capital increases.

67-d) - A statement of activities

The purpose of this statement is to exhibit the organization's major current and future activities and the way they influence the overall business performance.

67-e) - Business financial projections for the next 5-10 years

Below, with the permission of the respective company, we have cited an actual 6-year statement of projections for AU Inc.

	YEAR 1	YEAR 2	YEAR 3	YEAR 4	YEAR 5	YEAR 6
Number of employees at USA headquarters	90	100	120	120	150	150
Number of employees in main campus in Europe*	200	310	400	400	400	400
Employees at Distance Learning Centers	2,000	4,000	8,000	16,000	16,000	16,000
Projected number of stud. on Euro resort-campus	2,000	3,000	5,000	5,000	5,000	5,000
A.) Revenue from on campus tuition in Europe	$16,000,	$24,000,	$40,000,	$40,000,	$40,000,	$40,000,
Number of countries Ariston will have presence in	5 Countries	10 Countries	20 Countries	25 Countries	30 Countries	40 Countries
B.) Revenue from Distance Learning Centr.	$240,000*	$480,000	960,000,	1,200,000,	1,440,000,	1,920,000,
C.) Total Direct Revenue (A+B)	$256,000	$504,000	1,000,000,	$1,240,000	1,480,000	$1,960,000
D.) Direct Delivery Cost 30% of total revenue	$76,800,	$151,200,	$300,000,	$372,000,	$444,000,	$588,000,
E.) GROSS PROFIT FROM OPERATIONS	$179,200	352,800	700,000,	868,000,	$1,036,000,	$1,372,000,
F.) Operating Expenses 30% of total revenue	$ 76,800,	$ 151,200,	$ 300,000,	$372,000,	$444,000,	$588,000,
G.) Miscellan. Expenses 10% of revenue	$25,600	$50,400	$100,000	$124,000	$148,000	$196,000
H.) Total Expenses (Lines F + G)	$102,400,	$201,600,	$400,000,	$496,000,	$588,000,	$784,000,
I.) Profit from Educational Operations	$76,800,	151,200	$300,000,	$372,000,	$444,000,	$588,000,
J.) Housing revenue (# of stud.x $4,000.)	$8,000,	$12,000,	$20,000,	$20,000,	$20,000,	$20,000,
K.) Grand-Total EBITDA	$84,800	163,200	$320,000,	$392,000,	$468,000	$608,000,
L.) Return On Investment of $1 Billion based on EBITDA	8.40%	16.30%	32%	39.2.%	46.80%	60.8.%

67-f) - A statement of fair evaluation of operations, assets and profit

Here we should utilize experts to put together such statements. A list of capital equipment, machinery, furniture and land are some of them.

67-g)- A financial portfolio including all types of stocks, bonds, mutual funds and other

If we have or plan on issuing such instruments they should be listed here. If we already have them, we should show their performance for the last three years. If we are a start-up we should project how such instruments are expected to "behave."

67-h) -Investment instruments

What type of investments we are after, how we make them and how successful we have been, should be enlisted herein.

67-i) - An MD&A (Management Discussion/Analysis) of financial conditions / results on operations

This is not common but if we incorporate it into our Business Plan it could make a difference.

67-j) - Consolidated and/or Reconciliation statements (for existing entities)

Our CPA and /or CFO should put together these statements; not an easy task.

67-k) - Conformity with GAAP provisions

This is only an attestation that we have followed the commonly accepted guidelines and principles.

67-l) - With public companies, SEC regulations and compliance-types of stock

By submitting such attestations we are strengthening our position about the business and the way it is headed. The fact that we follow SEC regulations and comply with all regulatory guidelines definitely adds more validity to what we present in our Business Plan.

67-m) - Annual Financial Reports (for existing entities)

All organizations are compelled by law to comprise and submit to the appropriate authorities what is called: End-Of-The-Year Financial-Statements. We should provide such submissions from previous years, or if we are a start-up we should pledge that such statements will be provided and submitted according to the requirements of the law.

67-n) - Treasurer's reports (for existing entities)

A Treasurer should provide her/his report every month or quarter, never later that one year. The report is presented for approval, and if approved is consolidated with bank statements and incorporated along with the rest of the financial statements that should be included in the Business Plan. A treasurer's report lists the starting balance, the expenditures, the income and then the ending balance. It could be written on letterhead with the words "Treasurer's Report" on the top.

67-o) - Audit reports (for existing entities)

Same as with the Annual Financial reports presented above

67-p) - If applicable, a statement of Fiduciary Net Assets

If our organization or an officer of the organization has fiduciary responsibility, it should be shown here. The terms "fiduciary," "fiduciary assets," "fiduciary fund," and "fiduciary activity" may be used in general purpose Federal financial reports to characterize only fiduciary activity as defined in the standard.

More information regarding all statements shown herein could be found in:
Federal Accounting Standards Advisory Board
441 G Street, NW, Suite 6814
Mailstop 6K17V,   Washington, DC 20548,
Telephone (202) 512-7350   www.fasab.gov

We need to take the information outlined above very seriously. For some of these we have provided samples in the Appendix section. We strongly suggest that a CPA or a CFA should be engaged in putting together such statements. The information is highly specialized and one improperly composed statement or even an unrealistic number may discourage investors or bankers to proceed.

67-q) Supporting documents

Any documents that could strengthen our position should be enlisted either here or in the appendix. Such documents may include: Letters of recommendation, personal resumes, job descriptions, personal financial statements, credit reports, letters of reference, letters of intent, letters of commitment, leases, contracts, other legal documents, and anything else of relevance to the Plan.

68. Budgeting and funds needed

In item #29 above we discussed the importance of financial statements. Here we will address the role budgets play in a business and why it's important to incorporate them into a Business Plan.

In short, a budget is a futuristic financial plan. It's mainly expressed in monetary terms and covers investments, revenues and expenses. A budget, depending how elaborate it is, might provide a forecast of revenues expenditures along with how an organization is expected to perform financially if certain strategies, events or plans are carried out successfully; and finally a budget could allow for comparisons between the planned or expected and the actual data. Budgets usually cover from one to ten years in the future. Well organized companies comprise several different types of budgets, i.e. fixed or static, variable or flexible and also revolving budgets.

A budget in addition to revenues and expenses could also include "funds needed." Especially with start-ups or with companies that are growing, "funds needed" is a common item or possibly a whole segment of it.

In conclusion, a well-organized and presented Business Plan should definitely include a well-designed and presented budget.

69. Types of costs

Information regarding total costs will be included in the financial statements. Here we are concerned with the specific types of costs. For the record we should be showing:

a) Fixed expenses
b) Variable costs
c) Semi-variable costs or expenses

Fixed expenses are usually expressed as a total, while the variable costs are expressed per unit. The semi-variable are the ones that give us the most trouble, but we should be able to demonstrate them accordingly. Once we have mentioned and recorded these three major categories in the respective schedules, we should next show how they affect the bottom line and the organization's ROI. Additionally, we could show the action (s) we are taking to manage such costs and expenses properly.

70. Start-up costs/Investment

Even if you have been in business for many years it's always advisable to keep track of the initial start-up costs and investment. This is even more important if we are a kind new in the business. Why should we have this information shared? Obviously our competition may have been in business for just about the same number of years. Showing what our initial costs and investment were, people can look into how we did it, what it took and how significantly have we grown the initial investment.

71. The Break-Even-Point, the Payback Period and the Net Present Value

All three are vitally important elements of a Business Plan. Let's explain the meaning of each and then show how they should be used.

<u>Break-Even-Point</u>: Is a financial-business instrument that shows the point of sales where a company neither generates a profit nor suffers a loss. It's expressed in units or dollar values.

<u>Payback period</u>: Represents the amount of time it takes to recuperate the initial investment of a business; is expressed in time i.e. years.

<u>Net Present Value</u>: A concept that calculates the current worth of a future payment or receipt. Now that we confirmed our understanding of these three concepts, we should have no problem incorporating them into the business plan. For instance, if the initial investment is 10 million US dollars and the yearly net profit is one million, one may conclude that the payback period is 10 years. It appears to be correct; however from the moment you introduce the NPV of the annual receipts on one million, you will find out that you need more than 10 years to "Break-Even." Of course you have to have a rate of inflation for the calculation of the NPV.

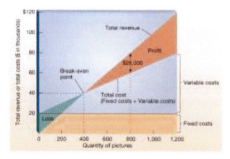

72. Make-or-Buy decisions

Organizations constantly are dealing with this dilemma. That's what we addressed in outsourcing as well. Obviously to do this properly we need to know the different types of costs, mentioned above, and their behavior. In reference to the Business Plan, all we need to demonstrate is that regarding out products we do run a "Make-or-Buy" analysis. This ensures people that indeed we run a well-managed and organized operation that is conscientious about costs, which in turn affect the selling price customers pay, our competitiveness and ability to present a viable organization.

73. ND-NC-NC Agreement

The acronym **ND-NC-NC represents NonDisclosure-NonCompete-NonCircumvent,** is commonly known as NDA

An NDA is a legal document between at least two parties that outlines confidential material, knowledge, or information that the parties wish to share with one another for pre-specified purposes, but restrict access to third parties. It's a contract through which the parties agree not to disclose information covered in the agreement, to outside sources.

A NonCompete usually is a clause within a NDA contract. It could be a contract all on its own. In a NCA one party, usually an employee or a seller or a party to a transaction agrees not to pursue the same or similar profession or trade in competition against another party. Usually a period of time, a radius and a consideration is stated in the NCA, amongst other important clauses.

A NonCircumvent agreement is drawn to protect sensitive and crucial information revealed during a business transaction. It generally provides that each party shall use the other party's information only for the purpose of pursuing a business relationship between the parties. In the event the parties elect not to pursue the business relationship, neither party shall have the right to make any use of the other party's information. It is often part of a non-disclosure agreement, NDA.

Not all companies have ND-NC-NC agreements, but if we do we should make sure that they are demonstrated in our Business Plan. By doing this, we convey the impression that we protect our interests and of course those of our investors.

NDA

NOTES

Project Management

PROJECT MANAGEMENT

74. The Business Plan is a Project

Putting together a well organized and developed Business Plan that tells a compelling story about our business is indeed a Project. Therefore Project Management principles should be deployed. A project is defined as *a continuous endeavor that has a clearly definable objective, must meet certain specification criteria, consumes resources and operates under time, funding and quality constraints; has a starting and finishing date and requires coordination, orchestration and synergy.*

In a Project we can identify several major/important elements, two of which are:

- The Milestones
- The Deliverables

On page #16 we stated the five sections of our Business Plan; obviously these are equivalent to **"Milestones."** *Introductory-basic topics / Marketing Considerations / Operational Requirements / Financial-Capital Requirements / Project Management*.

The specific tasks within each Milestone are equivalent to **"Deliverables."** Therefore, addressing the Business Plan from the Project's point of view is logical and equitable. Well, if we examine the definition of a project stated above, we shall see that it could also apply as the definition of a Business Plan.

At some point, all organizations deal with projects. Introducing a new product or entering a new territory or building a new facility, could be addressed in the form of a project. Reorganizing the office, rearranging the physical setting of people, departments and desks, could be another project. Given that one way or another we always are involved in projects, it would be nice to reflect that in our Business Plan. More specifically, a Business Plan should have a concise list of all projects the organization is involved in. Actually such list should include: All completed projects for the last five years, all current projects and their degree of completion and of course any and all future projects. That's usually done in a Project Portfolio presented next.

75. Project Portfolio

A Project Portfolio refers to a collection of all projects, programs and others works that could be grouped together to facilitate effective execution of projects as they relate to organizational strategic plans. For an organization that constantly gets involved in projects, it is advisable that a Project Portfolio is comprised. By incorporating the Project Portfolio concept into our Business Plan, we demonstrate that we comprehend the significance of it and we took the time to address it. This makes our organization appear highly knowledgeable and competitive. As stated above in # 74 the Project Portfolio should incorporate all past projects we performed in the last five years, all current projects and any future plans about new projects.

76. The role of the Project Manager and Scope of project

Now that we have defined "Projects" and "Project Portfolio" we could move on to something more specific. The role of the Project Manager resembles that of the orchestrator or coordinator. Just like an orchestra conductor coordinates, synchronizes and knows every instrument-player in the orchestra, Project Managers are aware of every "player" of every activity at any given time. They know where everyone and everything should be, any time during the execution of the project. By the way, for that we deploy tools we will address next.

Project Managers don't only know what we just demonstrated above; they also perform another, possibly more important, function. They constantly are reminded and keep others "on their toes" about the Scope of the Project. Having the Scope of the Project, continuously in front of you keeps you on target. We have seen Project Managers become overwhelmed with the daily activities of the project, thus they lose direction or sometimes even the Scope of the project. In our Business Plan we should assure the public that we don't fall in the category. On the contrary, our Project Managers know the Scope of the Project, keep it in front of them and they remind others to do the same. This way, we rest assured that the Scope is reached. And all that should be clearly demonstrated in our Business Plan.

Define the project scope: In defining the project scope we attempt to identify all the activities and functions that need to be performed, the project assumptions, the constraints and management functions in order to ensure that all requirements are in place, to successfully complete the project. By defining the project scope we ensure our stakeholders that the project will be completed on time and within the pre-specified budgetary constraints. This is an excellent element to be included in our Business Plan..

77. Develop the Project Plan

A Project Plan integrates and consolidates all of the subsidiary management plans and baselines from the planning process and includes: Scope baseline, scope management, change management, human resource requirements, costs, other resources, training needs, funds required, and risks involved. In addition it outlines the major stages a project goes through, such as Planning-Executing-Monitoring/Controlling-Closing.
In preparing our Business Plan we should make reference to these concepts. Such action enhances the appearance of the Business Plan and makes it more welcome to the public.

78. Project stakeholders

A project stakeholder is any party that has either a direct or indirect interest in a business or project. Stakeholders are classified into internal and external. As internal we understand the ones who come in direct and continuous contact with a business. Such factors may be: employees, owners and managers, board of directors and investors among others. On the external category we have society, government, employees' family members, the immediate-surrounding community, customers and competitors. Can you tell the difference between the two categories? It's mainly the immediacy and direct contact that make the difference. A well-organized Business Plan should make reference to the specific kinds of stakeholders who affect the business, or are affected by the business, either favorably or unfavorably. The graph below clarifies what we just described.

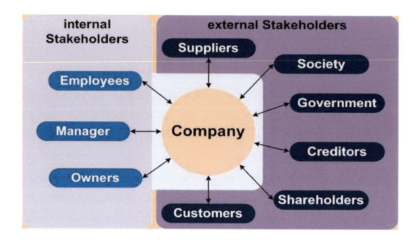

79. ID activities and their duration, WBS and deliverables

Now that we completed the project scope we could move on to identifying the specific activities that need to be performed for the completion of the project. This is done in phases. First, we try to identify the major components of the project. Next, we should estimate the time it should take to complete each component. For instance, if we are building a new office or factory, in the first stage we may include all activities associated with the design of the building, such as drawings, verification of them, approval and validation. Next, we should estimate how long it should take to do all this. As third phase may be obtaining permits from the appropriate authorities, i.e. building department, fire department, meeting city codes e.t.c. Once we have identified all activities we then group them together in some logical and procedural order. That's called Work-Breakdown-Structure or WBS. In other words, related activities are placed under the same major category. And then, within each category we identify the specific tasks, or otherwise called "the deliverables." Showing all this in our Business Plan, we convey the message that we definitely know what we are doing and where we are headed.

80. Develop the HR Requirements and the Project Schedule

In order to complete a project we need resources and the most important of all is the human talent or HR resource. It is the most significant resource, not only because it costs usually the most, but mainly because of its subjective nature. We can easily "manage" buildings, machinery, and equipment; but we can't say the same with our human resource capital. In order for someone to understand the difference, let us present the following comparison. If we placed 10 machines in our production environment, all 10 of them could be set to work exactly the same, produce an exactly equal amount of output, same exact quality and performance. If we placed 10 people in a production line, what guarantees do we have that they will give us the same-exact output as the 10 machines would above? None. Why? Because of the human factor that inserts a subjective element to the equation. Now, once we come to the realization that the HR factor is different from other resources, we stand a much higher chance of addressing it properly. Once we understand the sensitivity of the HR factor, we could proceed with the next steps. Such steps include, identifying, recruiting, attaining, training and developing our HR; and this should be performed an on-going basis.

Next, we should schedule the various activities or different projects. Scheduling is complex. There are so many variables that "enter the equation" it's almost pathetic, but definitely confusing, if you don't know what these methods are. Prioritizing projects and then scheduling the specifics, is a lengthy process. This is not easy. However by showing in our Business Plan that not only we are concerned with such issues but we know how to address them, makes us look really good in the eyes of potential investors or the public, in general.

81. Project Management and Communication

The sooner we come to the realization that the greatest cause of most problems, personal or business, starts with the way we communicate, the better off we will be. First, it's what we say and next, and most importantly, it's how we say it. People have "selective hearing" and they hear-understand what they want to hear or understand. We all do that, some more intensely than others. But we have all done it. Therefore communicating tactfully and effectively, becomes an important endeavor in the implementation of a project. We should come to the understanding that there should not be a "one size fits all" approach to our communication. As it was stated previously, with people we have the subjective factor; we have the personal idiosyncrasies that are so unique and particular with each person we communicate with. That's why we have developed various communication techniques that will be presented soon. For the time being, what we need to understand is that the art of communication should be as individualistic as the person's fingerprint. Once we come to this realization we stand a much higher chance of succeeding in our communication process. And that should be reflected in our Business Plan.

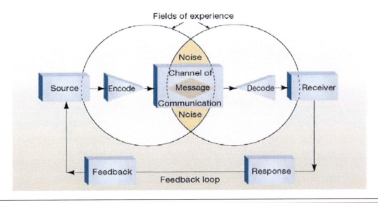

82. Estimate Resource Requirements, Project Budget and Cost Estimates

By definition, a project consumes resources and refers to future events. Since resources are usually scarce, it is advisable that we plan for them. Given that we are referring to future events we can only estimate them. Let's take each of its three components separately.

a) **Estimate Resource Requirements**: That's about all we can do; estimate/approximate.
Since we are dealing with future events, we can't calculate the resources needed with 100% accuracy. That's why we deploy all the different estimation or forecasting methods we have available to us. Such methods may be classified into quantitative and qualitative.

b) **Project Budget**: We have already established that with projects we are dealing with futuristic events. Also we have determined that projects require resources. One of the most effective ways of addressing both of these concerns is through the Project Budgeting Process. Here we try to estimate resources, but it's done in a formal and somewhat scientific way. We accomplish it via the budgeting process. We have already addressed the budgeting process earlier; that was an overall budget design for the organization. We are not contradicting or diminishing the need for it. All we are saying here is that along with the overall corporate budget, we should comprise a budget just for the project(s) we are working on. Such project budget is part of the corporate budget. This way we demonstrate that we don't only have a master budget for the organization, but we do the same for each smaller component of it, such as a project.

c) **Cost Estimates**: Given "a" and "b" immediately above, it's rather obvious that we have to estimate the costs of a project. If we don't do that, we won't be able to establish the Project Budget. In estimating costs, again, we have several different techniques that we deploy. Covering such techniques is not a concern at this time. It's important that we understand the significance of determining the type, estimating their size and lastly incorporating such cost estimates into the Project Budget. By doing that and clearly demonstrating it on the Business Plan, we appear highly sophisticated and our Business Plan looks more complete and consequently more convincing.

83. Plan Inputs, Tools & Techniques, Outputs

If anyone examines the PMI manual (PMI stands for Project Management Institute) will repeatedly find reference to "Inputs-Tools & Techniques-Outputs." This is nothing else but a methodology or an approach followed, in order to address these three important elements. We know that in everything we do there is, Input, Process and Output. PMI also examines the significance of "Tools & Techniques," meaning, when we process the Input or the Output, what techniques do we deploy? What methods do we utilize? PMI provides for it. All we need to do is apply it. As far as the Business Plan is concerned, we should make sure that we demonstrate that indeed we follow the PMI process. PMI is a reputable organization and showing that we abide by its guidelines can only help.

84. Project Network

Networking is one of the most exploited concepts in business today. It has been used by architects, doctors, business managers, engineers, academicians, attorneys, accountants and marketers, to mention a few users. Just about every profession or industry uses the term in some capacity.
In telecommunications or IT, figure A, reflects the interconnection of computers and work stations, in order to operate our business more effectively. So we have a "Network." More specifically:
In information technology, networking is the construction, design and use of a Network. This includs the physical arrangement, the selection, the placement and use of telecommunication and computer software for using and managing the Network and the establishment of operation policies and procedures related to the network.

In IT a small Network generally consists of two or more computers that are linked in order to share resources, exchange files, or allow electronic communications. The computers on a network may be linked through cables, telephone lines, radio waves, satellites, or infrared light beams.
In business figure B, we have connected people or departments represented by people, so that they may communicate more effectively. So we have another "Network." Wikipedia describes Business Networking as '*a socioeconomic activity by which groups of like-minded businesspeople recognize, create, or act upon business opportunities. A business network is a type of social network whose reason for existing is business activity*. There are several prominent business networking organizations that create models of networking activity that, when followed, allow the business person to build new business relationships and generate business opportunities at the same time. A professional network service is an implementation of information technology in support of business networking. Many businesspeople argue that business networking is a more cost-effective method of generating new business than advertising or public relations efforts. This is because business networking is a low-cost activity that involves more personal commitment than company money. Business networking can be conducted in a local business community, or on a larger scale via the Internet

Figure A   Figure B

Business networking websites have grown over recent years due to the Internet's ability to connect people from all over the world. Internet companies often set up business leads for sale to other companies looking for data sources.

In sales or job searching, figure C we have individuals or groups of people getting together to network in order to consummate a sale or find a career. So this is another form of a "Network."

Networking during the job search process is a powerful way to meet new contacts and to advance your job search to obtain the career you want.

How does all this relate to our Business Plan? Easy. We use the term Network in all aspects and forms described above.

Therefore we should let the public know that we have IT Networks, we have Business Networks and that we take advantage of the latest networking techniques and social media.

Figure C

85. Develop the project team and assign responsibilities

The benefits of a TEAM mentality and effort are rather obvious. The intent here is not to convince anyone on the advantages of it. Rather, we would like to remind ourselves that letting the public know that we believe in and operate under the Team frame of mind, is important. The acronym below demonstrates the significance of the Team mindset.

    T-*ogether*
    E-veryone
    A-*chieves*
    M-*ore*

Along with the composition of teams comes our responsibility of assigning specific tasks to the team members. Just putting a team together without specific objective and a time table, is a lost cause. We will address the training needs of a team at a later point.

In conclusion, we identify the various teams we assign their responsibilities and they "go to work." So, what do we do with it? Again, as in all previous cases, we tell the public that we operate our business cultivating and developing Business Teams. In doing that we should address the difference between teams and groups. We should make it crystal clear to our readers that we cultivate and promote the mentality of Team.

The table below clearly demonstrates our extended experience in converting "groups" to "teams." It's worth noting the fourth phase which is our invention. Our experience has shown us that after the "Norming" phase it's advisable to reconsider the previously assigned roles and possibly re-assign.

85-1 GROUP TO TEAM PROCESS

PHASE	CHARACTERISTICS	QUESTIONS	LEADERS' ACTION
1. Forming	Identification Introduction Excitement	What	Identify members' skills and capabilities Calm members down Take time to know members
2. Storming	Difference of opinion Conflict over tasks Arguments	Who	State and follow objectives Stick to your plan. Teach how to use conflict as opportunity
3. Norming	Understanding Relationships are formed Agreements are reached	How	Assure understanding of agreements. Establish basics for team behavior Set standards for excellence
4. Reforming	Restructuring-reassigning Finalization of roles Clear responsibilities	How and who	Reinforce commitment and loyalty Reallocate responsibilities and accountabilities Finalize agreements
5. Performing	Performance Results Cohesiveness	Who, what, how, why and when	Guide members, become a source of "know how" Build trust, loyalty and cohesiveness Reward for excellence
6. Adjourning	Fulfillment Enjoyment Disbanding	Is client happy? What is level of acceptance?	Audit process and members' performance Reevaluate members' behavior and stress lessons Adjust standards and roles for next assignment

86. Risk Management, Quantitative & Qualitative Analysis, Monitor & Control Risks

Risk Management is a science by itself. Many universities offer degrees on the subject, meaning its importance is paramount. Therefore, we will not attempt to address the subject in its scientific sense; rather we will stress the significance of incorporating such subject in our Business Plan.
More specifically we should be doing the following:

a) Mention that with avery action we take in our business there are associated risks and that we are equipped to handle them. We have the experts to identify risks and mitigate them.

b) Demonstrate that we are aware of the most important or effective Quantitative and Qualitative techniques to address such risks. In our Business Plan we should enlist two or three such techniques used in the past or even currently.

c) Monitoring and Controlling Risks, is a whole different aspect. In our Business Plan we should clearly demonstrate that we have not only identified risks, but we have ways of dealing with them and through the Monitoring phase we follow the progression of the risk (increasing-stagnant-decreasing.) In concluding this segment, we should also demonstrate the ways we deploy in controlling such risks. Again, we should cite 3-4 Risk-Controlling techniques here, as well.

87. Risk & Uncertainty

In dealing with the subject of "Risks" one needs to understand the difference between risk and uncertainty. Both appear to mean the same and indeed they have overlapping areas. However, from the business perspective as risk we understand an unfavorable event whose probability of occurring can be calculated with a great degree of accuracy. For instance, when a bank issues a loan there is a risk for the recipient of the loan to not be able to fulfill her/his responsibility, i.e. to repay the loan. However, the probability of defaulting on a loan can be calculated with a great deal of accuracy. We have historical data which may be deployed to calculate such risk. On the other hand, uncertainty is defined as the state of having limited knowledge where it is impossible to exactly calculate the existing risk and its future outcome. As it's shown in the graph on the next page, uncertainty could be viewed as a more general set of events, but from the moment we can calculate an uncertainty with some degree of precision we then move it into the risk circle.

88. Risk Register, Management and Response

Once we can calculate the probability of occurrence of an uncertain event, thus it's classified as risk we should look into ways and techniques we have in dealing with it. The graph cited next,

covers such techniques. We have risk:
A) Acceptance
B) Avoidance
C) Reduction
D) Transfer

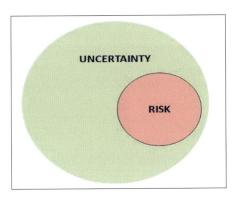

Risk Register acts as a log or a repository of all risks the organization is facing. In doing that we perform risk assessment, risk impact, counter measures and of course we identify the risk owner. Typically a risk register contains:

- Complete description of the risk
- The impact should this event actually occur
- The probability of its occurrence
- Risk Score (the multiplication of Probability and Impact)
- A summary of the planned response should the event occur
- A summary of the mitigation (the actions taken in advance to reduce the probability and/or impact of the event)
- Risk owner
- Contingency plan

Conclusion from the above: By showing all this information in our Business Plan we appear to be well equipped to handle the situation and readily available to anticipate any and all uncertainties.

89. Procurements, Acquisitions and Outsourcing

A well-organized Business Plan should address these crucial functions. Briefly we will cover the basic meaning or functionality of these terms.

a) **Procurements**, refer to the purchase of any and all items needed in a business

b) **Acquisitions,** first we need to realize that it is a wider concept that procurements. Then acquisitions refer to initiation of the need, design of the approach, development of the process, testing and verification of it, contracting and/or producing the item needed, the logistics of it and the distribution process. As we stated in the beginning, acquisition is a much more complex function and we need to reflect that in our Business Plan.

c) **Outsourcing,** is the process of contracting an outside organization to perform a process previously executed internally. Such process may include the production of a part or a component or even a service, like payroll. The most common example of payroll outsourcing is the issuance of paychecks by an outside organization like ADP. Companies outsource production of products or services for various reasons, some of which may include: Cost reduction, expert talent utilization, access to more knowledge, unwillingness or inability to expand to accommodate the production of said product or service and of course all that is performed with the ultimate goal to improve profits. If outsourcing is sent to another country, the preferred term is "offshoring."

In outsourcing we set evaluation criteria that we utilize in order to select the best organization we will outsource to. Such criteria may include: Reliability, consistent quality, price, on-time delivery, years in business, primary business, company reputation, technical expertise, knowledgeable management and industry complaints to mention a few.

In executing these functions effectively we request/perform the following:
a) A letter of intent
b) A RFI and RFP = Request For Information and Request For a Proposal
c) Due Diligence
d) Vendor Evaluation and Selection Form
e) Execute a Contract
f) Address HR Issues, including employee transfer, responsibility and liability
g) Logistics on Warehousing and Distribution
h) Vendor Benchmarking
i) Customer Satisfaction Survey
j) Reporting and Communication Methods
k) Press Releases
l) Negotiations and Renegotiations
m) Exit Strategy

Obviously all this is needed to be shown in our Business Plan so we can demonstrate that we are well equipped to handle this delicate but important function

90. Mergers and Acquisitions

Let's begin with the definition of both:

A Merger is combination of two organizations into a new one.

An Acquisition is the process by which the stock of a corporation or the assets of a company are transferred to a buyer, usually another corporation or company. In short, an Acquisition is a scientific and complex process, not a transaction.

Acquisitions are inevitable in the business world. Actually, certain businesses are in the business of "Acquisition." Unlike product or service purchasing, the "Acquisition" of a business involves mega million transactions. Acquisitions involve at least one seller and one buyer. Each has its own motives and goals. The seller wants the highest price possible, while the buyer wants to pay the minimum amount. The seller wants to base the price on "potential" and on the intangibles of the business, when the buyer is basing the offer on depreciated-discounted value of the organization's assets. Not an easy process to negotiate. That's where the terms "friendly or hostile" take-over come from.

Just like the vendor evaluation above, here too we go through some processes and documents:

a) What documents we ask for; financially we should ask for balance sheets, income statements, cash-flow statements, expenditure statements, payroll statements etc
b) How many years back should we go with these documents
c) The timing of the Acquisition
d) How to calculate the true value of a business
e) The NPV and the ROI methods
f) Find out why the seller is selling
g) Putting it all together

Now that we addressed the "Mergers and Acquisitions" concept, if you are interested in its specific elements, you may examine the following 16 pages. Portions of these pages may be included in a Business Plan only if you are involved in a major Merger or Acquisition.

Enjoy,

A Comprehensive-Master Business Plan

Mergers & Acquisitions

The following 16 pages are exclusively devoted to the specific issues that should be explored when a Merger or an Acquisition takes place.

The process is straight forward and easy to follow. For every question shown in the first column, we give a rate between one and four (1, 2, 3, or 4) in the fourth column. Periodically we add the points and transfer them throughout the entire process. At the end we sum-up the total points. The final number gives us a good idea of where we are headed, along with which area is doing better that the rest. By the same talking the process will point the areas where the company is performing poorly.

Mergers and Acquisitions checklist

QUESTION	LOOK FOR	Y/N N/A %, $	SCORE 1-4	Comments
Basic Issues				
Organizational Chart	Is there an organizational chart in place to demonstrate the type of organizational structure?			
Board of Directors	Obtain names, titles, CV's for each. Such info could be on their web			
Major clients	Who are they? ID 3-4 of them			
Major competitors	Who are they? ID 3-4 of them			
Last Merger, Acquisition or Divestiture	Any Mergers or Acquisitions in the last five years. Hostile take-over or traditional?			
Patents, Trademarks, Goodwill	What patents/Trademarks they own? What year are they in? Value of Goodwill, its percent to total assets and Net Worth			
Intellectual Property	What is its value? Is it realistic?			
Types of stock issued	Common, Preferred, Treasury, Class A, B			
Bonds outstanding	FV, Maturity, Interest, Coupons, etc			
Dividend distribution	Any dividends in arrears, cumulative			
Warranties and guarantees	Determine extend of liability			
Executive Compensation	How reasonable is it in relation to industry averages			
Legal structure of seller	Is it a corporation, LLC, Partnership, etc			
Number of employees	How many employees total and what is the ratio of professional to blue collar			
Employee turnover ratio	Compare ratio to industry average			
Physical environment	Cleanliness, "OSHA" regulations or equivalent, overall ambiance			
ISO certified	What specific ISO certification they have			
Corporate strategy and vision clearly defined	Obtain details about the company's strategy and a copy of its vision			
Company strengths	What areas the company has a comparative advantage			
Potential threats	Find out the possibility of new entrants			
Is there a list of ALL assets Tangible (Fixed-Current) Intangible	List of fixed assets recorded with proper authorities			
Book Value vs Market Value	What depreciation methods are used How much if the "Accumulated Depreciation" account			

QUESTION	LOOK FOR	Y/N NA %$	SCORE 1-4	COMMENTS
Percent of sensitive/high value assets	Physical security, Controls, Locks, Assigned Responsibility			
Identify what controlling mechanisms exist to protect sensitive and highly valuable assets	Document the type of physical controls, if any; identify person (s) responsible and accountable for them			
Are information assets protected and appropriately classified	Are sensitive data adequately protected from disclosure, modification, theft or destruction			
Inventory of assets has been effectively conducted and updated regularly	How are assets inventoried, how frequently and by whom			
Information security policies	Obtain copy of policy, if any			
Data confidentiality/integrity	Identify policy and consequences if it is bridged			
If such policies exist, are they distributed to all, updated regularly and understood by all	Obtain assurances/evidence on all three issues: Existence……………………………………………………………………………………… Updated………………………………………………………………………………………… Understood……………………………………………………………………………………	Y/N Y/N Y/N		
Ensure information security policies are effectively communicated	Discuss with management their strategy for communicating security policy Review new-hire security training programs and how they ensure compliance Find out how changes to the policy are reviewed and communicated to employees Interview employees from different business divisions to assess their understanding of security policies			
			___/ 120	Cumulative ___/ 120

QUESTION	LOOK FOR	Y/N N/A %, $	SCORE 1-4	Comments
Finance				
Bylaws & Standing Rules regarding finances	Find out the corporate policy about the way finances are maintained. People involved, responsibilities			
Board minutes regarding finances	- All expenditures approved, ratified and recorded in executive board minutes - All authorizations have receipt/bill attached			
Financial Secretary Reports	How frequently are they filed? Monthly? Obtain a statement			
Treasurer Reports	Same here			
Annual Financial Report	Obtain an audited copy			

QUESTION	LOOK FOR	Y/N NA %$	SCORE 1-4	COMMENTS
Audit Reports	How frequently are Audits performed? Semiannually? ……………………………………………………………………… Quarterly? ………………………………………………………………………			
Receipts/Deposits agree with ledger & register	Look for discrepancies			
Income received matches deposits recorded in checkbook register, ledger and treasurer reports	Look for discrepancies			
Cash receipts used	What method do they have in recording cash receipts and the amount they represent? Is it reasonable?			
Deposits and checks written	Who has authorization to sign checks? The president, treasurer and one other officer? - Recorded in checkbook register - Recorded in ledger in proper columns - Agree with treasurer reports			
Verify income received and recorded	-Income received matches deposits recorded in checkbook register, ledger and treasurer reports -Check to see if amount shown on first bank statement (adjusted for outstanding checks and deposits) corresponds to the starting balance recorded in checkbook register -Ending balances (checkbook register, ledger and treasurer report) agree with last bank statement			
Ledgers, authorizations and bank statements	-Receipts/Deposits agree with ledger and the register-Authorizations match checks written-All bank statements reconciled since last audit by treasurer and one other person			
Cash Verification Forms	Do they use certain forms for it and if so who authorizes them?			
Cancelled checks, including voids and NSF	Do they maintain a log? Ask to see it			
Budget (s) ……………………… Last Audit Report ……… Ledger …………………………….. Checkbook register…………………………	Date and person who performed it			
Bank statements, bank books and deposit slips	Is there a match?			
Workers' Compensation Annual Payroll Report form	This report will tell you plenty about the company			
If a US company and if required Other countries ask for equivalent forms	- IRS Forms 990/990EZ …………………………. - IRS Form 941 …………………………………. - IRS Form 1099 ………………………………… - State Form RRF-1………………………………. - Other forms as you deem necesary…………			
Account compliance	Do the accounts comply with requirements for external scrutiny?			

QUESTION	LOOK FOR	Y/N NA %$	SCORE 1-4	COMMENTS
Budgets	-Are annual budgets prepared and approved to cover both income and expenditure? -Is performance measured against budgets at regular intervals?			
Checks, balances and who performs them	-Are regular checks made to ensure records are accurate? -Are checks made by someone other than the original recording officer?			
Expenditure handling	-All expenditures approved/ratified in association minutes -All expenditures approved and recorded in executive board minutes			
Ending balances	See if checkbook register, ledger and treasurer report agree with last bank statement			
			___/92	Cumulative ___/212
QUESTION	**LOOK FOR**	**Y/N N/A %, $**	**SCORE 1-4**	**Comments**
Year-end wages/salaries	Detail on accrued wages at your yearend			
Basic financial statements	Balance sheet Income statement Cash flow statement Retained earnings statement			
Other year-end statements	Accounts payable listing at your yearend (open invoices that have not been paid Unpaid Vacation and Sick Hours Detail on Deferred Revenue Year-to-date General Ledger Trial Balance at year-end			
Significant Leases, Contracts, and other Agreements	Who are they with, when they expire, what are the consequences for early termination			
Bonds	If the co. has issued bonds, find out bond maturity date, interest paid (how much and how frequently) right to convert to common stock or repayment schedules			
Stock-shares	Types of shares issued -Common -Preferred -Treasury -Other types if any			
Dividends	Are they declared and paid every year? Are there any in arrears? Any dividends accumulated over the years?			
Payroll taxes	Payroll Tax Returns for all four quarters of your audit year			
A/P	Paid and Unpaid Vendor Invoices Is the preparation of payments undertaken by someone other than the authorizing officer?			

QUESTION	LOOK FOR	Y/N NA %$	SCORE 1-4	COMMENTS
A/R	-Aging of accounts, terms for collection -Are incoming receipts banked promptly and regularly			
Safe boxes and valuables	-Is the safe custody ensured for all valuables held on premises? -Are keys of safe or cash box signed for?			
Additional financial Statements	Along with the basic statements ask and inspect SEC documents (Annual reports, 10-Ks, 10-Qs, Proxy statements, Stock offerings			
Major reserves	Analyze last 3 years reserves, i.e. returns, warranties			
Non-recurring charges	Analyze any unusual and non-recurring charges; when and why they happened			
Prepaid accounts	Obtain a list of prepaid and deferred assets for the current period and last 3 years			
Inventory and audit reports	Obtain the last 3 years inventory reports and audits; look for unusual recordings			
Sales data	Analyze Sales Returns & Allowances in relation to overall sales			
			___/ 68	Cumulative ___/ 280
COGSold	Obtain and analyze sales, gross margin analysis by product and product line			
Factory Overhead	Analyze operating expenses and overhead costs by department and for the entire co.			
Consultants	Obtain a list of consultants used in the last 3yrs, how much they paid them and the type of service they provided			
Parent/Subsidiary	If it exists investigate intercompany transactions, profits-losses etc			
Product trends	Analyze volume trends (increase/decrease) and find out the reasons for such trends			
Financial commitments	Find out the type and size of financial commitment to: Leases, claims, litigation, severance agreements, joint ventures agreements, letters of credit, Swaps, etc			

QUESTION	LOOK FOR	Y/N NA %$	SCORE 1-4	COMMENTS
Treasury	Any and all debt agreements for: Public or private loans Bank debt committed facilities Line of credit Detail of unamortized debt issuance costs Agreements to convert, issue or exchange stock			
Financial risks	Obtain a copy of all insurance policies, carriers, coverage type, limits, premiums, deductibles and expiration dates			
OSHA /other such organizations	Obtain a copy of all OSHA citations and abatement information Any industrial hygiene reports			
High value property items	Obtain a list of all extraordinarily expensive assets, i.e. airplanes, yacht, luxury cars,			
Taxes – Federal	Obtain copies of: -Financial statements – last 5 yrs -Tax returns-last 5 yrs (Domestic & foreign) -Reorganization, acquisitions, tax rulings -Tax deficiencies or ongoing tax disputes, statute of limitations -Tax attributes for carryover of loses, capital loses, credits and tax basis of assets -Intercompany transfers of assets/liabilities -Treatment of foreign exchange gains/loses			
Taxes - Local / State (as applicable)	Obtain copies of: -All locations and activities in each location -Truck delivery logs and summaries (3 yrs) -Schedules for payroll, sales receipts -Net operating loss schedule detailing the losses by state, year incurred and used -Any pending refund and the reason for it			
			___/48	Cumulative ___/ 328
Sales Taxes	Obtain copies of: -Sales and tax returns for last 5 years -Customer invoices -States/countries co. is registered to sell -Open audit listings detailing the issues, jurisdiction, status and amount at issue			

QUESTION	LOOK FOR	Y/N NA %$	SCORE 1-4	COMMENTS
Property Taxes	Obtain copies of: -Fixed asset value & tax liability per facility -Tax bill showing taxes paid/outstanding -Tax assessments on appeal, if any			
Payroll Taxes	Obtain copies of: -Agreement if 3rd party does the taxes -State deposits -Payroll tax returns for 3-5 yrs -State unemployment compensation -Executive retirement plans			
Value Added Taxes "VAT"	Obtain copies of: -All locations domestic and foreign -Markets where to co has no physical presence but does significant business -VAT returns per country for the last 5 yrs -Correspondence with tax authorities			
Treasury	Obtain a copy of all debt agreement: Private debt Public Debt Any revolving line of credit			
Determine if external security reviews are conducted	Identify if they ever used independent evaluators to determine the validity of their security program			
Determine the frequency and revision of changes on to the security policies	Discuss with sellers their strategy for reviewing the security policy Identify a change or two and ask for specific evidence on how they implemented them			
Identify the sellers' commitment to information security	Identify individuals with explicit assignment and acknowledgement of information security responsibilities. Then interview these individuals to confirm information provided by the seller			
Are information assets properly recorded, protected and classified	Find out how, ask for records			
Determine if an inventory of assets has been effectively conducted	Find out how frequently they identify and record such assets.			
Identify what controls exist to protect sensitive assets	Look for technical and physical controls Find out if the custodians and users poles are played by the same person			
What policies exist for releasing such assets	Obtain a copy of the policy-procedure			
			___/ 48	Cumulative ___/ 376
Determine if employees are aware of security controls	Interview employees to see what their awareness levels are with regard to physical security policies			
Determine if separation exists between public and private areas	What controls exist to separate delivery and loading areas from private access areas			

QUESTION	LOOK FOR	Y/N NA %$	SCORE 1-4	COMMENTS
Determine if hardware maintenance policies exist	What controls have been implemented to ensure availability of systems			
Verify existence of Change Management (CM) program and ensure adherence to CM procedures	Obtain Change Management Program Documentation Obtain evidence that demonstrates request, approval, development, QA, staging, and production release changes.			
Verify that Service Level Contracts (SLC&A) and other Agreements have been defined, actively monitored and reported to management.	Request copies of SLC&As Request reports from activity and capacity monitoring			
Ensure service level escalation procedures exist	If need be, can service be escalated? Obtain evidence of previous instances of escalation through a ticket tracking system or status reports along with the reason why such escalation was needed			
Confirm that a business continuity plan exists to support business critical functions	Failure to provide adequate backup systems in the event of a disaster poses a risk to the business operations, communication and functionality			
Verify that a high-level business continuity plan has been documented to address critical functionality	Request copy of high-level Business Continuity Plans (BCP). Request copy of Disaster Recovery Plan.			
Is there a contingency strategy	Request evidence of a backup strategy that includes both critical systems, employee desktops, and employee functions			
Evaluate the network security controls to ensure adequate management of network devices and protection of data transmission	Failure to properly secure network devices or data being transmitted over the network poses a threat of disclosure, alteration, or destruction of information assets			
Are there any external and internal security controls	Work with Security Operations Center to identify and isolate IP segments for external mapping Discuss with seller any outbound filters that take place at the network level Document how internal events are monitored and logged			
		___ /44		Cumulative ___ / 420

QUESTION	LOOK FOR	Y/N N/A %, $	SCORE 1-4	Comments
Organizational issues				
Organizational Chart	Find out their organizational structure and obtain an organizational chart			

QUESTION	LOOK FOR	Y/N NA %$	SCORE 1-4	COMMENTS
Annual Plan/Forecast	Ask for the Master production Schedule (MPS) and identify the methods they use to forecast demand			
List of facilities	Identify the types of facilities, their size, capacity and value			
Overall Business Continuity Plan	Find out if they have a plan that explains how the business will perform even after a major disaster			
List of pending legal matters	Are there any law suits (individual or class action)			
Employee List (name and address)	The list of employees will help you determine the true "Labor Cost" The names and addresses will keep the seller "honest" to give you only actual employees			
			____/ 24	Cumulative ____ 444
Policies and Procedures				
Employee manual	Obtain a copy; it will give you a good understanding of the company's culture			
Human Resources/Hiring Policies	Ask to interview the HR department; find out how they go about recruiting people			
Union shop	Are your employees unionized? If yes, obtain a copy of all grievances past and present. The specific type of complaint (s) and the status of them i.e. solved, pending,			
Physical Safety Procedures	If OSHA is applicable look for compliance. If not look for the equivalent organization of the respective country to see if physical safety is indeed a priority			
Employee turnover statistics	-Find out the employee turnover ratio. It will tell you plenty about the company. -Compare it to industry average			
Training type, level and frequency	Find out if an internal training program exists, who attends it and how frequently people have to go through such training			
List of business suppliers, customers, 3rd party logistics and indirect partners	Obtain a list of all vendors for the last 5-7 years; same with customer list. Third party logistics and any and all partners, current or past			
Business/Data flow diagrams	Obtain any and all diagrams that reflect business operations, and the way data flows			
Outline of all services and product offerings	Make a list of all products/services the seller offers			
			____/ 36	Cumulative ____/480

QUESTION	LOOK FOR	Y/N N/A %, $	SCORE 1-4	Comments
Information Technology / Security				
Physical Security Controls (locks, badges, cameras, guards, segregation by job function, etc.)	How does the company secure all such concerns			
Data Center Physical and Environmental Controls Overview	What policies exist, obtain a copy			
Asset Management (hardware, software, owner, custodian)	Look for leasing contracts, their duration, cost and penalties for early termination			
Network diagrams	Who is responsible for their maintenance			
Virus and Malware Protection	Identify antivirus and other protection the company has			
Information Security Awareness Training	Who offers it, who attends and how frequently			
Password Policy for workstations, servers, network devices	Who secures the network system; How			
Data Retention / Destruction	How long the organization keeps the data. Five years, 10, 15?			
Event Monitoring and Log Collection (network, host)	Who monitors, what happens in anomalous situations			
Operations Monitoring	What operations are monitored most, by whom and how frequently			
System and Data Backup	How are data backed-up. How long do they keep them			
			___/ 44	Cumulative ___/ 524

QUESTION	LOOK FOR	Y/N N/A %, $	SCORE 1-4	Comments
Miscellaneous concerns				
My impression of the work-place	Physical work environment, ambiance, cleanliness			
Board of directors	CV's for each			
Organizational culture	What are the determinants of their culture; what shapes it			
Leadership, style, effectiveness	What Leadership style are they following			
Social responsibility	Are they adhering to adequate levels of social responsibility? How? Write specific examples			

QUESTION	LOOK FOR	Y/N NA %$	SCORE 1-4	COMMENTS
Legal compliance	Degree of compliance to local, national and international standards			
Country tariffs, quotas if any	Does the country have any quotas and/or tariffs that may affect the sales			
Political system of the country they are in	What is the political and economic system			
Government stability and future outlook	How stable is the Government. How frequently they hold elections in that country (foreign)			
Does the business have a comparative or absolute advantage over its competitors	Identify both: The Absolute and The Comparative advantage			
Decision making process	How are major decisions made? Collectively …………………………… Authoritatively ……………………………			
Does vision and mission collaborate with strategy	Obtain copies of all three and analyze them			
What is the long-term outlook	Prior to sale, how did they see the next 10-15 years			
Where is the industry headed	What is their feeling about the way their industry is going			
Policies, procedures and regulations	What major policies have they changed in the last 2-3 years			
Change	How do they go about change? Do they plan or react to it?			
			___/ 68	Cumulative ___/ 592

QUESTION	LOOK FOR	Y/N N/A %, $	SCORE 1-4	Comments
Quality				
Level of Quality	What 6Sigma level are they at? Ask for proof. When did they arrive to the level of 6Sigma they claim?			
MBO	Are they following the MBO approach?			
MBWA	Same here			
SWOT / SCOT	Same here; ask for some evidence on the SWOT analyses (4-5)			
Span of Management control	The number of subordinates a manager has is critical to the way the business functions. Find out what is the average "Span-of-Control structure			
Distribution of authority	How is authority distributed; is it centralized or decentralized			
Innovation – creativity	Have they been encouraging Innovation and Creativity? Ask for evidence. What have their people innovated in; or created			

QUESTION	LOOK FOR	Y/N NA %$	SCORE 1-4	COMMENTS
Employment laws Employment-at-will	What employment laws do they have; such laws vary from country to country			
Internal recruiting	Do they promote from within or they usually go to external recruiters?			
Performance appraisals	-How are they done -Who does them -How frequently -Are they predefined -Do the employees know how they are evaluated			
			___/40	___/632
Handling stress	Stress and Burnout are common phenomena. How do they deal with them?			
Reward systems	In relation to appraisals, how do they reward their people? Ask for specific examples			
Conflict handling	Are there procedures to handle conflict?			
Capacity	Start with overall company capacity. Then ask for specific departments, processes or machines. Ask for proof.			
Use of robotics	Do they use robotics? What percent of total production?			
JIT	Are they using JIT?			
MRP I & II	Are they using an MRP system? Do they use a MPS? What is the time horizon for it?			
CRP	How do they Forecasting Capacity? Do they correlate it to MRP and Capacity covered above?			
BOM & BOL	Ask for samples of BOM and BOL			
Kanban	How is their production environment? Is Kanban obvious through visual cards?			
Kaizen	What C.I. programs do they have in place? Do their people go through some type of certification? If so what type? Ask for the last 5-7 Kaizen applications; who was involved, people, departments etc			
Strategic commitment to TQM	Find out the support Top Management provides to the implementation of TQM			
Outsourcing	How do they decide about outsourcing a product or service? What are the selection criteria in choosing a vendor? Do they go through the process of Make-or-Buy decisions?			
Benchmarking	Which company are they using as a Benchmark? How well are they succeeding?			
Cycle time	What is the cycle time for the major product (s) they produce?			
Company layout design	Blue prints and architects plans			
New product opportunity	How conducive is the market to new products?			

QUESTION	LOOK FOR	Y/N NA %$	SCORE 1-4	COMMENTS
QFD or House of Quality	Are they using this technique? How? How frequently?			
Robust design	Do they use it?			
Modular design	Do they use it?			
Work centers / cells	How are they designed? How efficient are they? Expert systems layout?			
Continuous Improvement	Remember that Kaizen was mentioned above. Here you ask for the overall company training and development plan. Ask they to provide you the next 3-5 years development schedule			
Empowerment vs Delegation	Find out what do they use mostly; -Empowerment -Delegation			
		___/92		Cumulative ___/724
TQM Tools used	What specific TQM tools are they using? What graphs are they deploying to achieve and maintain Quality?			
Flow Diagrams	Example			
Time Function Mapping	Example			
Process Charts	Example			
Learning Curve	Do they take the Learning Curve concept into consideration and if so how? Where?			
NPV	Same for NPV			
BEP	Do they know the BEP per product?			
Pay-Back period	Are they using it and how?			
Costs (FO)	Ask for a list of all major Fixed Costs			
Minimum wage	What is the minimum wage in the state/country they are in			
Supply Chain Issues-global	How do they deal with Supply Chain Management? What methodologies do they have in place?			
Vendor evaluation/selection	Ask for the top four (4) criteria they use to evaluate and select a vendor			
E-Commerce	Is E-Commerce applicable to business? If so, how are they using it? To what extend? Ask for a percent to total sales			
E-procurements	Same here			
Scheduling and Logistics improvements	What improvements have they implemented in this area in the last two years?			
Third party Logistics	Are they using third party logistics? If so in what areas?			

QUESTION	LOOK FOR	Y/N NA %$	SCORE 1-4	COMMENTS
Inventory control	How do they maintain inventory control? What methods do they deploy?			
Record accuracy-verification	How accurate are their inventory records? What is the main purpose for calculating inventory? -Corporate tax filling? -Corporate evaluation?			
Cycle counting	What is the cycle counting? -Seasonal? -Cyclical? -Periodic?			
End-of-the-year-physical inventory	How do they calculate it?			
E-counting of inventory	Do they use it?			
Inventory models used	Do they use models like the EOQ?			
Reorder points	Are they set, how, by whom			
Work order execution / prioritization	When multiple orders need to be processed how do they prioritize?			
PERT, CPM, GANTT	Are Project Mgmt. Techniques utilized? To what extend? Ask for samples of the tools mentioned			
			___/100	Cumulative ___/824
Maintenance / TPM	Ask for TPM programs, policies and then see how well they were followed. Ask for the last 2-3 years maintenance reports			
Reliability, Precision, Accuracy	Just like the previous item, ask for evidence. These three areas will tell you plenty about the company's operational efficiency. At this point you may want to ask for info on MTBF			
			___/8	Cumulative ___/832
Marketing				
Marketing Philosophy	Ask about the strategy they follow; are they into mass production and sale or they customize their sales? Are they using CRM?			
Company Core Values	What does the company believe in?			
Customer behavior	How do they monitor customer behavior?			
Segmentation and market size	Ask about their segmentation strategy; find out how they segment their customers /geographic areas			
Targeting/Is market fragmented	How effective is their targeting approach?			
Positioning	How do they position themselves in relation to the competition?			

QUESTION	LOOK FOR	Y/N NA %$	SCORE 1-4	COMMENTS
Pricing Is it affected by seasonal/cyclical	What pricing method (s) do they use? Cost plus, differentiation, leadership, mark-up, competitive, discounted etc			
Market development/barriers of entry	What do they do to develop their market share? Have they introduced new products or have they explored new territories?			
Brand Equity	Have they built a "Brand Equity" over the years? How well known their product is			
Price fixing	Have they ever been cited for "Price Fixing"			
Price war	Have they ever engaged themselves in a price war with competition?			
Marketing channels of distribution	How many channels until end consumer?			
Advertising/PR/ Publicity/Promotional budget	Find out how much they spend on these areas. Is it a fixed $? Is it a % of total sales?			
Does the advertising and PR program work?	How do you know? What matrix do you have in place to determine it?			
Product status	Have any products been discontinued or developed in the last five years? Which ones? Why?			
Problematic products	Have there been any product recalls in the last five years? Which ones? Why?			
Nuclear relationships	Have any of your products ever been used for nuclear purposes/facilities?			
			___/68	Cumulative ___/ 900

QUESTION	LOOK FOR	Y/N N/A %, $	SCORE 1-4	Comments
Legal				
Business certificate	Obtain a copy of the "Legal Form of Business" If a corp. ask for certificate of incorporation, If a partnership, ask for the contract etc			
By-Laws	a copy of the business By-Laws and the minutes for the last five years' meetings			
Public announcements	Obtain and review any announcements made in the last five years			
Claims and Litigation	Ask for a list of any and all: Lawsuits Claims Investigations Judgments (past or outstanding)Opinions of in-house or outside counsels			

Subsidiaries	Obtain a list of all current and past subsidiaries, percent of ownership (majority-minority interest) and any outstanding liabilities to them			
Jurisdiction	Obtain a copy of the jurisdiction the company and any subsidiaries are allowed to function			
Liens and other obligations	Obtain a list of all: Liens Mortgages Security interests Pledges Encumbrances against assets currently owned or to be purchased			
Warranties	Obtain a copy of the warranty policy A copy of any payments as a result of the warranty (last five years)List of recalls and the economic damage			
Acquisitions and Divestitures (A&D)	Obtain any such A & D made by the company and /or any subsidiaries. See if there is a continued liability			
Property	Obtain a list of all properties claimed by the company along with copies of deeds for them			
Intellectual Property	copies of all patented or otherwise owned IT Local or global :Patents Trademarks Copyrights Trade names			
IT Collaborations	List of all IT partnerships and/or alliances, along with agreements entered into on behalf of the company affecting Intellectual property			
Employee developments	Provide a copy of the employee confidentiality agreement and employee inventions			
Security	Provide evidence of the measures taken to protect all Intellectual property from been invaded by unauthorized personnel/competition			
Contracts	Obtain a list of all contracts regarding: Purchases Sales Consulting agreements Licenses Assignability of contract			
Employee claims	Obtain a list of: Paid claims to employees (5 Years) Pending claims to employees Individual or class action lawsuits by employees			
Representation	Obtain a list of any "Power of Attorney" given to a third party			
			___/68	Cumulative ___/ 968
Government compliance	Obtain a list of all regulatory reports and compliance status. More specifically ask for the following agency investigations, if any, or the applicable ones if foreign company: FCC ………………………………………………….EPA ………………………………………………….SEC ………………………………………………….OSHA ………………………………………………….EEOC ………………………………………………… ERISA			
			___/4	Cumulative ___/972

Appendices

A Comprehensive-Master Business Plan

> We suggest that these graphs should be incorporated in the Business Plan
> By incorporating them you demonstrate that you don't only present a theory about your Business Plan but you also have ways of tracking performance and expressing it pictorially.
>
> A. Gantt Chart   B. Interrelationships Diagram   C. Process Diagram

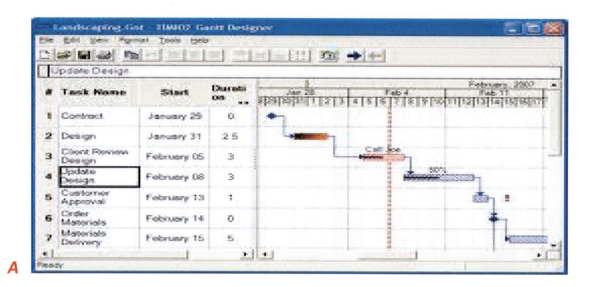

A Comprehensive-Master Business Plan

> We suggest that these graphs should be incorporated in the Business Plan
>
> D. Matrix Diagram   E. Decision Tree Diagram

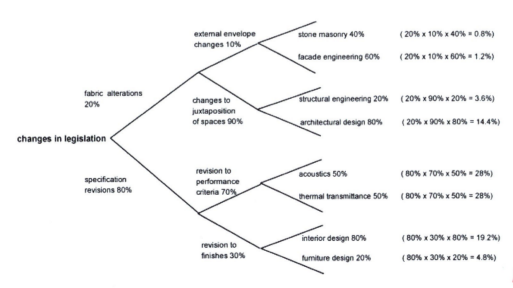

D

E

V

F. Network Diagram (P.E.R.T.), G. Bottleneck Diagram, H. Process Diagram

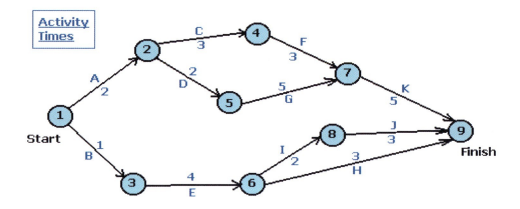

F.

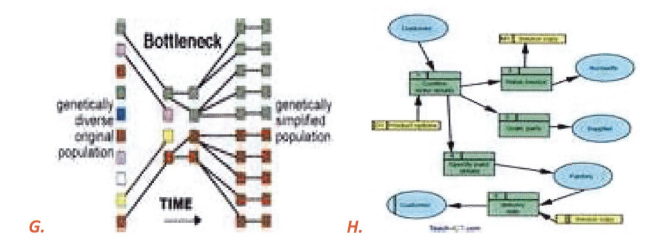

G. H.

I. Affinity diagram or Sticking notes diagram   J. Tree diagram with expected values

I.

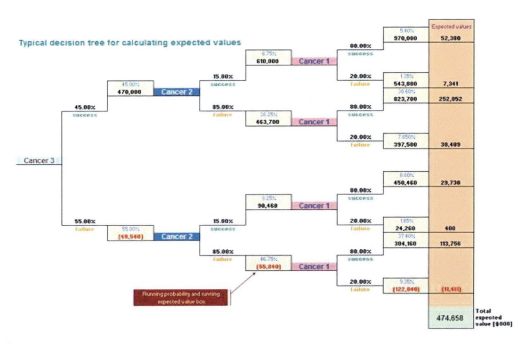

J.

K. WBS chart (Work-Breakdown-Structure)   L. Computerized flowchart

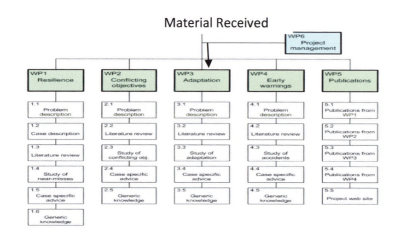

K.

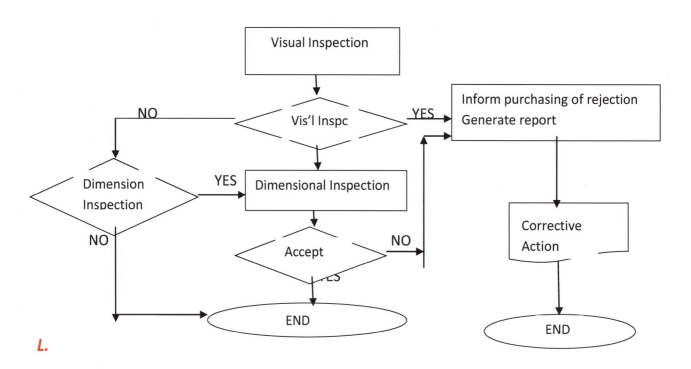

L.

TEAM MEMBER RELATIONSHIP AND EVALUATION

INSTRUCTIONS: First identify and list 10 people from your work environment and another 10 from your social environment. Next evaluate your relationship with them on the disciplines shown on the vertical columns on the top of the form. Your rating should be on a scale 1-10 with 1 indicating "the least or minimal" and 10 indicating "the most or the best". Five (5) and six (6) are not acceptable values. Work with 1-4 and 7-10.

	NAMES AND TITLES OF PEOPLE YOU WORK OR ASSOCIATE WITH …………………………………………………	1 TRUST	2 LEADERSHIP	3 SOURCE OF KNOWHOW	4 DEGREE OF LIKENESS	5 IS ACCOUNTABLE	6 IS SUPPORTIVE	7 TACTFUL COMMUNICAT	8 RELIABLE/ DEPENDABLE	9	10
1											
2											
3											
4											
5											
6											
7											
8											
9											
10											
11											
12											
13											
14											
15											
16											
17											
18											
19											
20											

M. Multiple trend charts, they help us determine direction and strength of relationships between variables *x* and *y*.

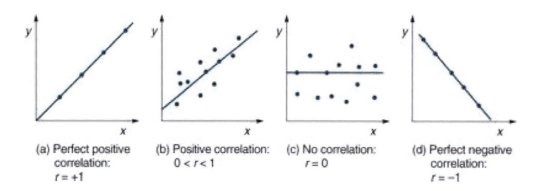

Organizational Stakeholders

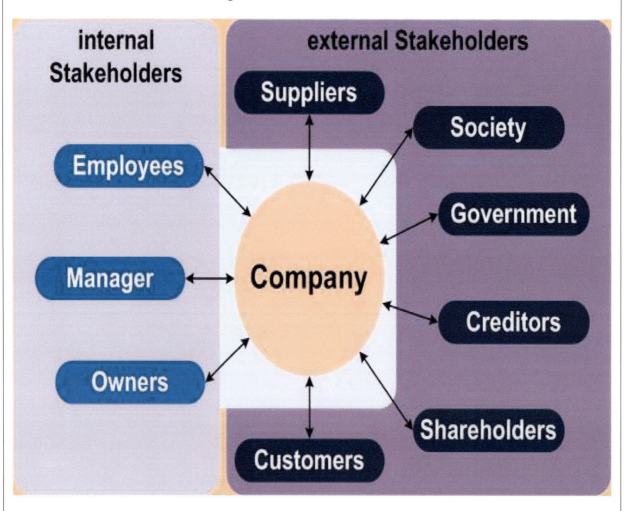

NOTES

N.

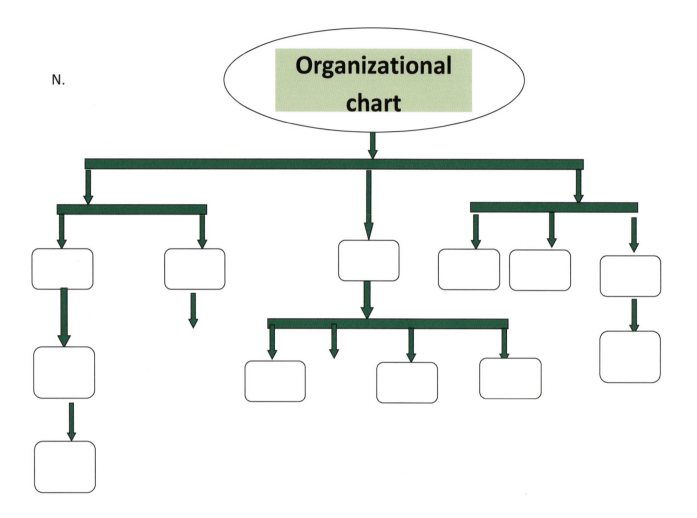

NOTES

O. STATISTICAL PROCESS CONTROL

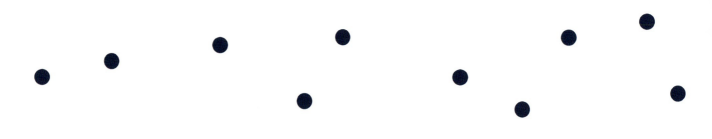

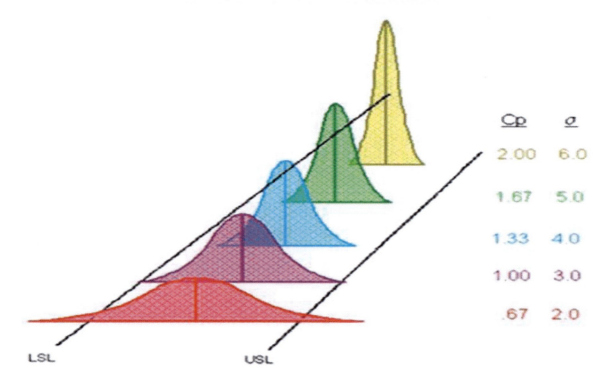

BALANCE SHEET   (Very simplified)
For XYZ Corporation as of 12-31-xxxx

ASSETS... **300**

    Current Assets... 120

        Cash................................... 10

        Accounts Receivable..................... 15

        Notes Receivable...........................25

        Office Supplies.............................. 5

        Merchandise 55

        Prepaid Expenses.......................... 10

    Fixed Assets... 180

        Buildings..........................40

        Machinery........................60

        Equipment......................50

        Land................................. 30

LIABILITIES...**200**

    Short Term Liabilities..80

        Accounts Payable.........................20

        Notes Payable...............................45

        Salaries Payable............................15

    Long Term Liabilities..120

        Mortgages......................................80

        Loans...40

OWNER'S EQUITY.. **100**

        Capital...70

        Retained Earnings........................30

INCOME STATEMENT (Very simplified)

For XYZ Corporation for the period of xx-xx-xxxx through zz-zz-zzzz

REVENUE 320

      Sales...250

      Commissions Earned............................ 50

      Miscellaneous Revenue....................... 10

      Interest Earned..................................... 10

COSTS AND EXPENSES 290

      Cost of Goods Sold 200

      Utilities... 20

      Rent.. 30

      Insurance... 15

      Admin Expenses................................... 25

NET INCOME... 30

CASH-FLOW STATEMENT

	Month 1	Month 2	Month 3	Month 4	Month 5	Month 6
RECEIPTS						
State Grant	$12,400	$12,500	$—	$25,000	$12,300	$12,600
United Way	9,450	—	9,450	—	9,450	—
Donations	1,430	2,000	4,300	1,200	1,200	1,200
Hourly Fees	2,450	2,500	2,200	2,200	2,200	2,200
Loan Received	—	—	—	12,000	—	—
TOTAL RECEIPTS	$25,730	$17,000	$15,950	$40,400	$25,150	$16,000
DISBURSEMENTS						
Salaries	$19,550	$19,550	$19,550	$19,550	$19,550	$19,550
Fringe	3,519	3,519	3,519	3,519	3,519	3,519
Rent	1,320	1,320	1,320	1,320	1,320	1,320
Legal	—	—	450	—	—	—
Debt Service	—	—	—	—	860	860
Capital Purchase	—	—	—	15,000	—	—
Insurance	1,800	—	—	—	—	—
Telephones	246	250	250	250	250	250
TOTAL DISBURSEMENTS	$26,435	$24,639	$25,089	$39,639	$25,499	$25,499
STARTING CASH	$15,450	$14,745	$7,106	$(2,033)	$(1,272)	$(1,621)
RECEIPTS	25,730	17,000	15,950	40,400	25,150	16,000
DISBURSEMENTS	26,435	24,639	25,089	39,639	25,499	25,499
ENDING CASH	$14,745	$7,106	$(2,033)	$(1,272)	$(1,621)	$(11,120)
GOAL – 30 Days Cash	24,639	25,089	39,639	25,499	25,499	

NOTES

MARKETING-SEGMENTATION BY GEOGRAPHIC CRITERIA

Key Segments	Period 1 ($m)	Period 2 ($m)	Period 3 ($m)	Period 4 ($m)
Segment A				
Segment B				
Segment C				
Other segments				
Total market				

Key Segments	Quarter 1 ($m)	Quarter 2 ($m)	Quarter 3 ($m)	Quarter 4 ($m)
Segment A				
Segment B				
Segment C				
Other segments				
Total market				

Sales Analysis (2012-2015)				
Years to end	2012 ($000)	2013 ($000)	2014 ($000)	2015 ($000)
Product K				
Product L				
Product M				
Product N				
Product O				
Total sales				

PRACTICE YOUR FINANCIAL NUMBERS HERE

A Business Plan should always be…….

A CHECKLIST OF BASIC ISSUES

AREAS OF CONCERN	Y-N N/A	COMMENTS
Legal name of business and DBA if applicable		
Legal form of business, type of corporation		
Address of main office and other locations, if any		
Address of registered officer		
Names and addresses of 3-4 main officers		
Names and addresses of major investors/shareholders		
Professional advisers		
Legal Adviser		
Bank and Banker's name		
Auditor(s) Internal-External		
Is there a Parent company involved		
Is company traded over the counter		
If YES, which exchange if not insert N/A		
Main telephone and Facsimile		
Main e-mail		
Website		
Are we on LinkedIn, Facebook, etc		
Name and address of other businesses owned		
Intellectual Property Registration		
Licenses owned by the business or shareholders		
Any additional information that we deem important		
Significant contracts i.e. leases, sales-purchase		
Types of Insurance		
Is our Strategy feasible		
Do we have verifiable Risk-handling procedures in place		
Is our Target Market defined adequately-satisfactorily		
Does the Plan tell a compelling story about our business		
Were _most_ people involved in composing the Business Plan		
Do we have a contingency plan for everything we plan to do		
How well do we know the business and the industry		
Do we have a long-term plan, not just our vision		
Realize that this Plan is a living renewable document		
ROI, EBITDA		
Other items we feel are important		

WORKSHEET

Finally, if we have any of the following we should include them in the appropriate place; for example:

- Any brochures and advertising materials that we developed
- Articles written in newspapers or magazines
- Photos of "before" and "after" (this applies mainly to existing businesses
- Industry studies done either by us or others
- Blueprints and architectural plans (what it would look like when is complete)
- Maps of the location (especially if traffic is a "plus" and the location supports that)
- Letters of support from future customers, especially if they are big customers
- Commitments made by vendors or strategic partners
- Any other materials needed to support the assumptions in this Business Plan

Next we have provided an outline of all elements explained herein.

The outline should serve as a compass for our actual Business Plan.
We should select and include only the items that pertain to our specific case.

MASTER BUSINESS PLAN OUTLINE

A. INTRODUCTORY-BASIC TOPICS

1. Executive Summary
2. Vision Statement
3. Mission Statement
4. Quality Statement
5. Code of Ethics
6. The Type of Business we are in and Market assessment
7. Our Products
8. Our competition and competitive edge -Feasibility Study
9. Strategic partners
10. Management team and professional advisors

B. MARKETING

1. What is our Marketing philosophy
2. Market Strategy, Market share, Growth strategies, PR, Advertising
3. Market analysis: Segmentation, Targeting, Positioning, Pricing, Demographics
4. Describe our target market and market niche
5. Overview of your products/services
6. What's coming next
7. Customer demographics
8. Where are our growth opportunities
9. Stages of market development
10. New Challenges
11. Industry trends: Can you perform a competitive-trend analysis on the following?
a) Product/service
b) Price
c) Quality
d) Image/style/design
e) Perceived value
f) Brand recognition
g) Customer relationships
h) Delivery time of product/service
i) Convenience of use
j) Credit policies
k) Customer/client service
l) Social consciousness
m) Product mix/line
n) Projected Market Share and Market Growth
o) Operational Efficiency, Effectiveness and Productivity
p) Operational Costs (high-medium-low)
q) Technological Competence-IT/Web
r) Patents/Trademarks/Copyrights

MASTER BUSINESS PLAN OUTLINE, continued

s) Creative ability
t) Innovative ability
u) SWOT or SCOT analysis
v) SWOT Chart
w) Competitive Analysis Chart

C. OPERATIONAL CONSIDERATIONS

1. Engineers and R&D
2. Benchmarking, ISO series
3. Learning curve
4. People, training / development
5. Risks
6. QC tools and Fish-Bone Diagram
7. Useful graphs and charts
8. Top-down/Bottom-up approach and Tall /Flat hierarchy
9. Layout considerations
10. Location concerns
11. Team building and self-directed teams
12. Core competencies
13. Outsourcing
14. Groupthink vs Brainstorming
15. Conflict resolution
16. Capacity concerns
17. Machinery and Equipment
18. Logistics, Supply-Chain Management
19. Policies, Procedures and Manuals
20. Forecasting
21. MRP / CRP
22. Scheduling: Forward-Backward

D. FINANCIAL CONSIDERATIONS

1. Overview of Financial statements and projections
2. Budgeting and funds needed
3. Types of costs
4. Start-up Costs and Investments
5. BEP, Payback Period & NPV
6. Make-or-Buy decisions
7. ND-NC-NC Agreement

E. PROJECT MANAGEMENT

1. Project Management and Communication
2. Estimate Resource Requirements, Project Budget and Cost Estimates.
3. Plan Inputs, Tools & Techniques, Outputs
4. Project Network
5. Develop the project team and assign responsibilities
6. Risk Management, Quantitative & Qualitative Analysis
7. Risk and Uncertainty
8. Risk Register, Management and Response
9. Procurements, Acquisitions and Outsourcing
10. Mergers and Acquisitions

12. The role of the Project Manager and Scope of project
13. Project stakeholders
14. Develop the Project Plan
15. ID activities and their duration, WBS and deliverables

16. The Business Plan is a Project
17. Project Portfolio

A note from the Author

Dear colleague

I sincerely hope you found this information useful and beneficial.

I would be delighted to hear from you.

You may contact me via e:aristonu@att.net

Your input will be

Warmly welcome
And
Greatly appreciated!

Printed in Poland
by Amazon Fulfillment
Poland Sp. z o.o., Wrocław